JESUS

CHANGED

EVERYTHING

JESUS

CHANGED

EVERYTHING

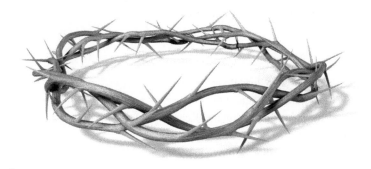

HE CHANGED HISTORY

HE CAN CHANGE YOUR STORY

ANTHONY F. RUSSO

Dedications and Thanks

To John,
A true friend for over thirty years.

To Joe,
My oldest brother and the one who first told me Jesus
Changed Everything.

And special thanks to Jim Holmes at GreatWriting.org,
Andrew Rappaport at StrivingForEternity.org and the
Christian Podcast Community, my early beta readers,
and my wife and co-host, Amy, wielder of
the editorial Red Pen of Doom.

CONTENTS

JESUS CHANGED EVERYTHING

You might be reading this book because I gave it to you when we met in a store or a coffee shop. Or maybe someone gave you a copy. However it came into your hands, let me say *I am glad we met. Thank you for taking the time to read it.*

Coffee shops, a delicious meal at a nice restaurant, work, and sleep are all the stuff of universal human experience. Life is full of those sorts of everyday activities. And while there are many good and happy events we have in common, pain and suffering are also part of life for all of us.

When the patriarch Jacob was asked by Pharaoh in Egypt how old he was, his answer wasn't a happy one: "The days of the years of my pilgrimage are one hundred and thirty years; few and evil have been the days of the years of my life. . ." (Genesis 47:9). Job—a man whose life has been regarded as the epitome of suffering for at least five thousand years—said, "Man is born to trouble, as the sparks fly upward." (Job 5:7).

If you and I asked a hundred people on the street what they're going through, we'll hear all kinds of hardships:

"I'm drowning in debt."
"I lost my job/can't find a job"
"I'm going through a divorce."
"I'm questioning my sexuality."

"I just got diagnosed with . . . and it doesn't look good."
"I've got a family member in jail."
"I'm addicted/I know someone who is an addict."
"Someone close to me died."
"I'm afraid."
"I'm angry."
"I've been depressed for a long time."

What about you? What keeps you up at night? Maybe you read something from the list above and thought, *Yep, that's me.*

Even if life is going great right now, there is still one inescapable reality in the distance: *One day you are going to die.* None of us knows when and there is nothing any of us can do to avoid it.

What about you?
What keeps you up at night?

Why do I start this book on such a somber note? Because in some respects, all of us are just trying to make sense of this world and figure out our part in it. And because whatever is going on in your life today, or whatever may happen tomorrow, I'm eager and excited to share good news.

JESUS CHANGED EVERYTHING!

It's true. No one can deny that Jesus Christ changed the course of human history. He changed how we reckon time—our very calendar is based on Him. He changed the world. How many thousands of hospitals have been built, bringing mercy and healing in His Name? How many schools established worldwide? How many widows cared for? Orphans adopted? Homeless and poor cared for? Jesus has changed the lives of millions, even billions, of people. And in 2005 He changed me.

The life, death, and resurrection of Jesus is the ultimate game-changer. He left the glories of heaven, took on flesh and blood just like us, and became a Man, fully God and yet also fully Man. His life, death, resurrection, and ascension to heaven changed everything. Because Jesus changed everything, Jesus changes everything.

Because Jesus changed everything,
Jesus changes everything.

For these two thousand years Jesus has been saving men and women who have made a complete mess of their lives. He's rescued drunks from the despair in their bottles and pulled addicts from the misery of their pills. He's changed men and women who were filled with lust, anger, hate, and violence to make them love again. He's given hope to the hopeless, comfort to the grief-stricken, and new life to those who were all but dead.

The Apostle Paul referred to Jesus' power to redeem and transform lives when he wrote,

Do you not know that the unrighteous will not inherit the kingdom of God? Do not be deceived. Neither fornicators, nor idolaters, nor adulterers, nor homosexuals, nor sodomites, nor thieves, nor covetous, nor drunkards, nor revilers, nor extortioners will inherit the king-

> dom of God. *And such were some of you.* But you
> were washed, but you were sanctified, but you
> were justified in the name of the Lord Jesus and
> by the Spirit of our God
> (1 Corinthians 6:9-11 emphasis added)

"And such were some of you," he says, as he reminds them how Jesus changed them completely, washing them in His blood, making them holy, and declaring them righteous before the Father. Paul had first-hand knowledge of Jesus' saving power. Before Jesus changed him, Paul was a member of the Jewish religious leaders, the Pharisees. In his zeal he grew to be a fierce opponent and violent persecutor of the first Christians. Then the Lord saved him, and he was never the same.

Jesus Christ has changed the lives of countless men and women, boys and girls, bringing them through every hardship and background imaginable. There is no life the Savior cannot save, no trauma the Prince of Peace cannot bring you through, and no sorrow He cannot replace with everlasting joy.

A CONTEST AND A QUEST

One would think that with such overwhelming proof of Jesus' power to save and to change, the world would flock to Him. After all, in 1848 reports that gold was discovered in California swept across the land, setting off what became known as the California Gold Rush. Hundreds of thousands of eager prospectors left everything behind in hopes of finding precious treasure. Well, for two thousand years the world has heard the reports: *Jesus is man's eternal treasure! There is ample treasure for all who come to Christ!* Instead of leaving everything to follow Him, most who hear the Good News just shrug their shoulders and stay home.

And yet, the world clamors for *something* to worship. The whole world is a contest of gods. Mankind has created thousands of gods to worship and philosophies to chase after. Why? Because the evils, the sufferings, the overwhelming beauty in this world, and our own God-given consciences point us to something more. All of us are on a quest for truth.

SEPARATING FACT FROM FICTION

My purpose in writing this book is to help you know Jesus. In order for us to know Jesus, we must separate fact from fiction. We can think we know Jesus, because of what we learned at church as a child or what we've heard about Him over the years, but if we are to know Jesus, we must parse truth from error, fact from fiction.

Consider this story of the famed novelist, Mauve Binchey. On a trip to the Holy Land Binchey visited the place traditionally believed to be where Jesus ate the Last Supper with His disciples. She thought she was going to see the room pictured in Leonardo da Vinci's famous painting, *The Last Supper*.

What Binchey did not know was that da Vinci's painting was only the expression of his artist's imagination. The original building was long gone by da Vinci's time. In fact, we have no idea what it looked like. What stands there now was built hundreds of years after the first century AD.

The novelist wasn't just disappointed. When she realized that the place she had traveled so far to get to did not match da Vinci's magnificent interpretation of it, she felt betrayed. Not betrayed by the artist, but by Christianity itself! Binchey felt betrayed because she failed to separate fact from fiction. To make matters worse, rather than own her mistake, she decided to completely reject Jesus Christ.

Did you catch the stunning irony of Mauve Binchey's story? This gifted writer used the mind God gave to research and write for a living. She used her God-given imagination, to create characters and detail their worlds. Binchey and her readers both knew that the scenes and stories were fiction, not at all reality. Yet she never stopped to consider that da Vinci did the same thing, only with a paintbrush instead of pen.

But Mauve Binchey's story is not just ironic. It's tragic. She applied her brilliant mind to research so many details, but failed to probe the most important truths in the world: the Person and Work of Jesus Christ. Instead, she rejected Him. Not because of anything He actually said or did, but because the facts did not match the fiction she had convinced herself was real. She deceived herself into believing the imagery of the great master over the incarnation of the Great Master.

What about you? Is it possible you have deceived yourself, that the picture in your mind of who you think Jesus is may not be Him at all?

Just because we may be sincere in our beliefs, our sincerity doesn't make them true. We can be sincere. . . and sincerely wrong.

Binchey's story proves the old saying that just because we may be sincere in our beliefs, our sincerity doesn't make them true. We can be sincere . . . and sincerely wrong. That may be OK for some things in life, like sincerely believing your favorite sports team is the best. But if we don't get it right on who Jesus is, we will regret it and suffer the consequences for all eternity.

That's why, of all the things in life that you and I could spend a few hours learning about, there is nothing and no one as important as Jesus. In this world we can either fool ourselves with wrong ideas about Jesus, or we will base our faith on the facts presented in God's Word.

I wrote this book to tell you that
He can do the same for you.

I wrote this book to tell you that He can do the same for you. God has always been kind and merciful to work in the lives of those who look to Him in faith.

IF JESUS IS TO CHANGE EVERYTHING, HE MUST HAVE EVERYTHING

But Jesus is not some self-help fix. We can't simply attach Jesus to our lives like a Band-Aid® over life's hurts. That is to dishonor Him worse than if we were to never come to Him at all. If Jesus is to change everything, He must have everything.

Imagine you needed heart surgery. You wouldn't say to the surgeon, "Doctor, I'll make you a deal. I'll lie on the operating table. I'll let you put me under

anesthesia. But I don't want you cutting me open."
Telling the doctor how to do his job would be crazy.
Unless the doctor intervenes and does exactly what he
knows is right you are the one who is going to die.

And yet, that's exactly what people try to do with
Jesus. People try to bargain with The Great Physician
all the time. How do they try to strike a deal with Jesus?
In their attitude towards Him they say, *Jesus, you can
bless me with good things, but don't tell me what I can and
can't do with my life.* I know because I did it for twenty
years. No, if Jesus is to change your life, if you would
know the Jesus of the Bible and not the Jesus of dead
religion or your own imagination of who He is. He must
have everything. No limits. No bargains.

What will you find in the pages of this book? If I have
done my job, you will find Jesus on every page. This
book is all about Him.

Are we going to cover everything? That would be
impossible. Jesus is God, infinite and eternal. All He is,
all His glory, is infinitely beyond our finite minds. The
Apostle John was one of Jesus' twelve apostles who
traveled with Him for the three years of His earthly
ministry. Look at what he wrote as he reflected on his
time with Jesus:

> And there are also many other things that Je-
> sus did, which if they were written one by one,
> I suppose that even the world itself could not
> contain the books that would be written.
> (John 21:25)

That's quite a statement, isn't it?

THE KING IS CALLING

And yet, by God's grace, we are not abandoned by our Creator. *You* are not abandoned by Him. Quite the contrary. The God of the universe, the One who the Bible tells us placed the stars and calls them by name, who hung the earth on nothing, and is sovereign over the kings and kingdoms of men and gives them to whomever He pleases, is calling you to Himself (Psalm 147:4; Job 26:7; Daniel 4:25)!

We have a lot to talk about, my friend, so let's get started.

A CONTEST OF GODS

Elijah was a man of God in the Old Testament, the writings in the Bible before Jesus' earthly ministry. He was a prophet, a man appointed by God to act as God's ambassador, preaching and warning the people to turn from their sins and turn back to God, or face the consequences.

In 1 Kings chapter 18 we read about the amazing confrontation between Elijah the man of God, and the 450 false prophets of a pagan god named Baal. Elijah challenges them to a contest. A contest of gods. Elijah invites them to the top of Mount Carmel and, well, let's let him explain it:

> *"Therefore let them give us two bulls; and let them choose one bull for themselves, cut it in pieces, and lay it on the wood, but put no fire under it; and I will prepare the other bull, and lay it on the wood, but put no fire under it. Then you call on the name of your gods, and I will call on the name of the Lord; and the God who answers by fire, He is God." So all the people answered and said, "It is well spoken."*
> *(1 Kings 18:23-24)*

This dramatic showdown did not end well for the prophets of Baal. After a long day of desperately pleading to their god for an answer, the skies were silent. Nothing roused their god, not even cutting themselves to get his attention. This went on for hours. Elijah eventually began to mock their god for not answering. *Shout louder! Maybe he's asleep! Maybe he's in the bathroom!* And still, no answer. Then it was Elijah's turn.

Elijah repaired the altar to the Lord that had been torn down and dug a trench around it. He cut up a bull and laid it on the wood on the altar. Then he instructed the prophets of Baal to drench the sacrifice with water. Then do it again, and once more after that. The sacrifice was soaked and the trench was filled with water. It would have been humanly impossible for it to catch fire. God's answer would have to be unmistakable.

Then Elijah prayed to the Lord, the God of Israel, to send down fire. The Lord answered immediately. Fire came down from the sky and completely burned up the sacrifice—the bull, the wood, the stone altar on which it lay, and every last drop of water. "Now when all the people saw it, they fell on their faces; and they said, 'The Lord, He is God! The Lord, He is God!'" (1 Kings 18:39). Elijah ordered the false prophets rounded up and put to death.

ELIJAH'S CHALLENGE IS OUR CHALLENGE

Why do I bring up this story? Because most people today don't realize they are in a modern-day contest of gods. They whole-heartedly embrace their spiritual beliefs and pit them against the Lord, who alone is God in heaven. They spend their lives praying to a god who doesn't hear them because he doesn't exist.

I once had a friendly conversation with a very nice

Hindu man. As we got to talking, he was so excited to show me photographs of his god at an elaborate celebration. There in the picture on his phone was a colorful statue, impressively ornate. But it was lifeless.

By the way, the idols that people choose to worship do not have to be carved with hands. Some people worship the earth. They believe the rocks and streams, the moon and stars. . . all of it is god. Billions of people worship gods of other world religions. And some people claim they worship nothing at all.

As you read through this book and see Jesus, I challenge you to think objectively about Him, and compare your own beliefs. Test what you believe against what the Bible says about God, Man, Sin, and the Person and Work of Jesus Christ.

How do you do that? Well, first you need to know what you really believe. Ask yourself: *What are the core convictions I base my life on? What do I think happens when someone dies? If there is a heaven, how does a person get there? And if there is a hell, how do they not go there?* Really think about it. It could take days, weeks, or even months. That's OK. Then, once you know what you believe, you need to evaluate it. Scrutinize it.

Think of it this way. Before a bridge is constructed, engineers rigorously stress test the design model. They want to find all the hidden weaknesses before it is ever built and people are trusting their lives to it every time they drive across it.

If you were to stress test your spiritual beliefs the way engineers stress test a bridge design, how would they hold up under the scrutiny? How do your beliefs hold up when loaded down by life? How have they supported you in recent years? When you really need your god, is he (or she, or it) silent, like Baal? Will what you believe about Jesus and what happens when you die comfort in your final moments on this earth and equip you for eternity? Don't wait to find out, it will be too late. Most importantly, will they adequately prepare you to stand before God—Elijah's God, the God of the Bible—the One before whom all of us, the Bible says, must answer and give account? Or will your beliefs fail you in the day of testing the same way the false god Baal failed his devoted-but-deceived followers?

STAR-STRUCK

I'll never forget the time I talked to a lady at work about her beliefs. We were both working at an old manufacturing plant in Louisville, Kentucky. She was outside on a cigarette break and I was out there to get some fresh air and sunlight, since most of the second floor I worked on had no windows. As we were chatting at the curb, the conversation turned to spiritual things.

As we were talking about her spiritual beliefs I asked her the fundamental question, "What do you think happens when you die?"

"I believe when I die, I'll become a star. We all become stars."

"Wow," I said, genuinely surprised at such a strange answer. I'd never heard it before and wanted to know where she got it from. "Is that something you read somewhere? What do you base your belief on?"

As surprised as I was by her belief, what came next stunned me even more. She said she came up with the idea herself. When I pointed out that she believed something with absolutely no evidence whatsoever of whether it was true or not, she agreed completely and saw no problem with that. She was totally fine staking her eternal soul on an idea she just made up out of thin air!

Whether you realize it or not, right now you are betting your life and your eternity on your beliefs. Are you 100 percent sure they are right? What is your proof?

CERTIFICATE OF AUTHENTICITY

When I bought my wife's engagement ring it came with a Certificate of Authenticity, a little card from an authorized and certified diamond institute ensuring that the diamonds in the ring were genuine. Years before that I bought my dad an autographed photo of his favorite guitarist, Chet Atkins. It, too, came with a Certificate of Authenticity. But there are also completely bogus certificates out there. Even today, forgeries in the art world and antiquities markets are big business. Prized paintings promoted as the works of renowned artists turn out to be fabulous, but worthless, fakes. And supposedly priceless ancient artifacts end up being bogus cons. Unsuspecting buyers are duped out of thousands, and sometimes millions, of dollars.

Jesus Christ is His own Certificate of Authenticity...He is God. He is the Second Person of the Trinity, God come to earth in the form of a Man.

What do art forgeries and not-so-ancient artifacts have to do with spiritual beliefs and Christianity?

~23~

Jesus Christ is His own Certificate of Authenticity. He Himself is His own proof that what He said and did are true.

Jesus' credentials are unquestionable. He is God. He is the Second Person of the Trinity, God come to earth in the form of a Man. He fulfilled hundreds of prophecies of His coming, including prophecies about what town He would be born in, when He would be born, that He would be crucified, and that He would rise from the dead three days later.

When Jesus began His public ministry, He healed untold numbers of deaf, blind, and the lame. He spent long days with crowds who brought people for Him to heal. He fed thousands with only a few loaves of bread and a couple of fish. And He raised the dead back to life. The Gospel accounts of Jesus don't even include all the wonderful, miraculous works that He did.

Then He was arrested on bogus charges, wrongly condemned to death, beaten, whipped, mocked and made to wear a crown of spike-like thorns, and crucified on a Roman cross, hanging there for six hours. The wrath of God was poured out on Him for sinners, exactly as the prophets foretold.

After His death He was buried and His grave was not only ordered sealed shut, but it was guarded by a dispatch of Roman soldiers. Nevertheless, three days later He rose from the dead. His grave was empty and He was seen alive by His disciples on numerous occasions. Everything happened exactly as the prophets had foretold and as He said it would.

And talk about scrutiny! Every recorded word Jesus said has been picked apart, doubted, and dismissed by countless scoffers and skeptics. Ever since the stone of

His tomb was rolled away at His resurrection, no stone has been left unturned trying to roll it back. Scholars have also tried, and failed, to say Jesus never existed. However much men try to discredit Jesus, not a single word or deed He did has collapsed under the scrutiny of His fiercest critics. We think "cancel culture" is new but people have been trying to "cancel" Jesus for two thousand years.

And yet Jesus remains the most talked about, the most written about, the most sung about, central figure in human history. There are millions around the world today who, like me, can say beyond a doubt that He changed their life. And there are millions more who came before us and are now with Him in heaven who rejoiced to say the very same thing.

...Nothing and no one has changed
lives, and continues to change lives, like
the Lord Jesus Christ.

Let's face it: All religions claim to be life changing. Beliefs like Islam, Mormonism, Jehovah's Witnesses, or atheism may even turn the most dishonorable scoundrel into an moral person on the outside. But nothing and no one has changed lives, and continues to change lives, like the Lord Jesus Christ.

QUEST FOR TRUTH

Look around and you'll notice there is a contest of gods everywhere in our culture. It's not just a contest. It's a quest. A quest for truth. It started the moment the serpent first tempted Eve in the Garden of Eden, causing her to doubt everything she knew about God. Ever since our first parents wandered away from God's truth, humanity has been on a fruitless quest trying to replace it with anything else.

When Jesus stood before Pontius Pilate, Pilate asked Jesus, "What is truth?" (John 18:38). He wasn't really searching for the truth. He was scoffing at the idea that truth even existed, blind to the fact that the Man standing accused before him was *the* truth, as we will see in the next few pages.

Even though there aren't many bookstores left these days, when I was in one recently it occurred to me that bookstores are kind of like secular temples, where seekers go searching for truth, asking the same question Pilate did.

Whether a person realizes it or not, anyone who doesn't know Jesus is grasping to find meaning, truth, and hope in this world. People rarely see their quest so clearly though. It's not like anyone walks up to the information desk and says, "Can you tell me where the book is that gives the meaning of life?" Given what's in most bookstores, it's probably a good thing they don't.

Sure, most go into a bookstore to find books about

stamp collecting, cookbooks, or other ordinary subjects. But people also go to bookstores to solve life problems like relationship issues or help to become a better person. Even scanning the rows and rows of weight-loss books is a person's way of seeking hope and help to become better (and lighter) than they are.

If someone went into a bookstore to find answers to life's big questions, where would they look for them? They would almost certainly seek it in the great minds of literature. But how much literature would they have to read before they find their answers, if they could? Is truth in art? Philosophy? What about all those self-help gurus? But if any of those people had real answers, why are new books with updated ideas constantly being churned out?

That day in the bookstore, as I walked around and reflected on the high-brow art books, and all that art evokes and tries to communicate about life, or the rows and rows of self-help books, philosophy, and spirituality/world religions, a mix of sadness and joy came over me.

"Lord," I thought, "thank You that I am a Christian."

That's not to sound arrogant. I'm not boasting that I'm better than anyone. I'm boasting in the miracle of God's grace to save a sinner like me. Here it is, almost twenty years later, and I'm still overwhelmed with gratitude that the Lord saved my life. I'm so glad He revealed Himself to me, convicted me of my sins, and impressed upon me my desperate need of Himself. I thank God that He led me to the truth. That is, He led me to Himself.

That's why I can't bear to think about how sad it must be to be a lost person earnestly trying to find truth in this crazy world. How tragic to go into a bookstore hoping to find real answers but coming away empty, or worse, with a best-seller that promises answers but only delivers tantalizing lies.

A few years ago, the same thing happened when my wife and I went into a small independent bookseller's shop in a quaint mountain town in North Carolina. This one turned out to be a mostly New Age / spirituality bookshop. The shopkeeper was very nice and greeted us as we entered. Her shop was clean and all her books were well-organized. Sadly, many of her books were New Age, Spirituality, and all kinds of philosophy and empty religion. There were books on Hinduism, mysticism, healing stones, Native American religion, etc., I don't recall seeing a single book telling about the hope that is found only in Jesus. After a few minutes we both walked out exhausted and a little depressed. We were both exhausted for anyone who might go in searching for truth and depressed that there were so many books, so many paths, and yet no light and no hope.

SEARCHING FOR TRUTH: SO MANY CHOICES

If you really think about it, searching for truth in a book-store is a depressing, hopeless endeavor on many levels.

For one thing, there are so many books to choose from. Solomon famously wrote, "Of making many books there is no end. . ." (Ecclesiastes 12:12). And to think he wrote that thousands of years before the printing press. Think how much has been written and published in just the last 600 years since Guttenberg's world-changing invention.

SEARCHING FOR TRUTH: WHAT IF IT'S NOT THIS BOOK?

One could spend one's whole life reading all kinds of ideas and philosophies, going broke on buying book after book searching for truth, and never finding it.

And what about the millions of books out there you'll never get to? What if the one book with real truth was the one that you never got to? What misery!

And what about all those ideas and philosophies? It wouldn't take long for you to discover they rarely, if ever, agree. One philosopher comes along with an idea about why the world is the way it is. A generation later another comes along and modifies it. A generation after that someone else comes along offering his own version and says, *No, no, no, the first two were completely wrong!*

SEARCHING FOR TRUTH: WHO IS RIGHT?

In the same way, suppose you read one book and take what that author tells you as truth. But then, further into your quest, you read another author, and he or she tells you the exact opposite. Both seem entirely plausible, but both are completely incompatible. Are you beginning to see the dilemma of it all?

And that assumes there are only two paths. What happens when ten authors disagree? Or twenty? Or a hundred? And now you must choose which to believe or be left to discredit the lot and start over.

Again, how sad and exhausting.

SEARCHING FOR TRUTH:
WHAT IF THE TRUTH IS NOT IN MY LANGUAGE?

What if the meaning of life isn't even found in your language? What if you spend your whole life reading books to find truth, only to somehow discover it was in some dusty old book on some high, out-of-reach shelf, on the other side of the world, in a completely different language?

SEARCHING FOR TRUTH:
THE ODDS ARE AGAINST YOU

Those are some of the dangers truth-seekers face if they set out to summit the Everest of this world's ideas. If they could read a hundred books a day, spending their entire lifetime looking for truth, they'd still die without knowing if they ever actually found it. That is, apart from the grace and mercy of the truth-revealing God who reveals Himself in the pages of His Word, the Bible.

THIS IS THE TRUTH, RIGHT HERE

How can I be so sure Christianity is *the* truth? Because, by God's grace, He opened my eyes to the truths in the Bible. The Bible is God's Book. It is the Word of God. Theologians call it God's "specific revelation" of Himself and the way of salvation. We can see glimpses of God's power and His attributes in creation, but nature can't show us Jesus or teach us how to be saved. Only the Bible can do that. In the Bible I saw that truth ultimately is not a book to read, it's a

Person to know and worship: Jesus Christ, the Son of God. Jesus declares, "I am the way, *the truth*, and the life. No one comes to the Father except through Me" (John 14:6, emphasis added).

I love bookstores, don't get me wrong. And, in many writings there is some element of truth. But only the Bible is God's truth for mankind. Only in the Scriptures of the Old and New Testaments is Jesus prophesied and the way of salvation revealed to us. The truth this world is desperate to find is in the eternal Son of God, the Lord Jesus Christ.

In AD 156, a bishop in Smyrna named Polycarp was martyred for his faith in Jesus. At his martyrdom he was offered one final chance to recant his faith in Christ and live. Instead, the aged and highly respected bishop replied,

Eighty and six years I have served Him, and He has done me no wrong. How then can I blaspheme my King and Savior?

Polycarp served Jesus for nearly a century and his dying words were to say that Savior had done him no wrong. I have only known Jesus for about fifteen years, but I can also assure you, "He has done me no wrong."

A Christian's testimony doesn't prove anything. People who believe a lie can believe it so sincerely it changes their lives. Being willing to die for a cause doesn't prove anything either. But how is it Jesus, an obscure Jewish peasant in the eyes of the world, has been credited with radically changing countless lives for two millennia? That fact doesn't prove Christianity is true either, but it should make us sit up and take notice. Something is going on here. Something is unique about Jesus. He is without a doubt the most remarkable Person ever to live. Surely, if you are a rational human being, all of this has to count for something worth serious consideration.

Baptist preacher Vance Havner summed it well,

> *You will find what you need in Jesus. Not in that book which you hope will reveal some magic open sesame on the next page. . .He is Alpha and Omega–and all the letters in between–so you need not go outside His alphabet to complete the wording of your life.*[1]

If you wish it were as easy as walking into a bookstore, going to the Information desk and asking, *Can you please point me to truth, so I can find eternal life?* Let me answer that for you.

Even the most irreligious bookstores on the planet will almost certainly have a Bible. Find it. Ask for it. Buy it. You will never spend better money in this world. Every dollar will be repaid to you ten-thousand times over. Then get alone with it. Ask its Author to open your eyes as you read it (John 16:13).

> *Even the most irreligious bookstores on the planet will almost certainly have a Bible. Find it. Ask for it. Buy it. You will never spend better money in this world. Every dollar will be repaid to you ten-thousand times over.*

1   Vance Havner *Day by Day: A Book of Bible Devotions* Fleming H. Revell Company. Old Tappan, New Jersey, 1953. Page 256. Or see http://vancehavner.com/devotion-of-the-day-497/

Do that, and I assure you, you will find the truth and the life you seek. It's all there, and more, because it is all in Jesus Christ.

WHAT ARE YOU LIVING FOR?

Where are you in your personal quest for truth? One way to find out is to get alone in this super-fast, noisy world, and ask yourself, *What am I living for? What do I believe?* Make a list of the things that really matter to you. What gets you out of bed each day? Our motives are the fuel in our tanks, firing up our engines each new day.

I once watched a documentary about a man who devoted his entire life to documenting the architectural details of every subway station in New York City. He spent decades filling hundreds of journals with meticulous notes and intricate sketches of every single station. Another man was so intelligent that he kept going back to college to earn advanced degrees. He'd become a doctor, a lawyer, a bio-ethicist, and still he was going back to earn more degrees.

The things that motivate us reveal who
we are and what we value.

Those men have motives few if any of us can relate to. Most people would say they live for family, for career success, or maybe some would admit they just want to "live it up and have a good time" while they can. People all have different motives, but one thing we all have in common is: The things that motivate us reveal who we are and what we value. After all, if it wasn't important to us, we wouldn't spend the time doing it.

WHERE DO MOTIVES COME FROM?

Here's another one of those truisms about people: We talk most about what we value most. That's why as I talk to people I listen for what is important to them. What is most important to a person will naturally come up in conversation. Let me give a real-life illustration of how this works.

One time I met a young man at a business networking event. It came up in conversation that he said he was a Christian. He seemed sincere, too. We talked more and agreed to meet for coffee.

The day for our coffee meet-up came. He was dressed in a smart dark blazer and was enthusiastic as he talked about being a marketing entrepreneur. I was impressed with the young man and his apparent business acumen. He said all the right things and had big plans.

Unfortunately for me, what I did not know until we really got to talking was that his "marketing business" was one of those multi-level marketing schemes, and that day I was his mark. Our meeting was so that he could try to recruit me into it his network.

The story continues. Although I was not at all interested in joining his network, I *was* interested in talking about the spiritual things we supposedly had in common. I soon discovered, however, that despite his earlier sentiments, he was more enthusiastic about the pyramid scheme he was caught up in than about the things of God. What was most important to him naturally came up in conversation. He was more motivated by the temporal affairs of this life than the eternal realities of the next.

This is a good time for us to ask: Where do our motives come from? God, in His Word, tells us. Our motives, He says, come from our hearts, the core of who we are. From our hearts, "spring the issues of life," the Bible says in Proverbs 4:23. And Jesus said, "out of the abundance of the heart his mouth speaks" (Luke 6:45).

What is in your heart? What does your heart inspire your mouth to talk about? Is it family? Sports? Politics? Living for the weekends? Is it money and earthly success?

Another story: I once met a very successful real estate agent, a real high performer. She boasted that before her feet hit the floor each morning, she would challenge herself, "Where can I get a new sale today?" She did not realize it, but in that one statement she revealed her heart: She was living her life for chasing after money.

"THE HEART OF THE PROBLEM IS THE PROBLEM OF HEART"

"The heart of the problem is the problem of the heart." In other words, every thing we do individually, or we see happening in the world, is the direct result of what is in our hearts.

Let's talk more about this idea of the heart. When I went to Uganda in 2019, I met a missionary, Abrie, from South Africa. Abrie is a broad-shouldered young man. He is very funny and also very eager for people to know Jesus. In his thick Afrikaans accent he would tell them, "The heart of the problem is the problem of the heart." In other words, everything we do individually, and everything we see happening in the world, is the direct result of what is in peoples' hearts. And what is in our hearts isn't as good as we think it is.

By God's grace, most people around the world do not wake up each day determined to deal drugs, traffic human lives, or lie, cheat, or murder. Still, because God made us, He knows our hearts. In the Bible God tells us important truths about our hearts:

- The thoughts of our hearts are "only evil continually" (Genesis 6:5).
- Our whole heads are sick and our whole hearts faint (Isaiah 1:5).
- Our hearts are "deceitful above all things, And desperately wicked" (Jeremiah 17:9).
- Jesus said that out of our hearts come "evil thoughts, murders, adulteries, fornications, thefts, false witness, blasphemies" (Matthew 15:19).

We may think we are good people, but God confronts us with the ugly truth. Our thoughts are futile, He says, and looks at our hearts and pronounces them "foolish. . .and darkened" (Romans 1:21). God sums it up by saying, "For there is no difference: *for all have sinned and fall short of the glory of God,*" (Romans 3:23, emphasis added). God's Word reveals the heart of the matter: None of us are the good people with good motives that we think we are. All of us have broken His laws. The heart of the problem is the problem of our sin-sick hearts.

OUT OF ALIGNMENT

Have you ever driven a car with its steering out of alignment? If you have, you know it acts like it has a mind of its own, and only ever wants to pull to one side. Left to itself, the car will drive itself (and you) right off the road. Until you can get to a mechanic to have the wheels realigned, you have to counteract the pulling by constantly correcting the steering wheel over to the opposite direction.

Our hearts are the same way. From the moment we are born into this world, our hearts are like a car that is permanently out of alignment. We only ever want to veer in one direction: Away from God, away from all that is holy and pure and pleasing to Him.

No matter how good we may appear on the outside, God has shown us that our hearts, those springs from which our lives flow, are utterly polluted with sin. Left to ourselves, our sin appetites would drive us headlong to our own destruction.

Getting back to my original question: *What are you living for?*

Three of Jesus' closest friends on earth were two sisters, Martha and Mary, and their brother, Lazarus. Luke, in his Gospel account of Jesus' life, writes about a day Jesus visited Martha's home.

> *Now it happened as they went that He entered a certain village; and a certain woman named Martha welcomed Him into her house.*
>
> *And she had a sister called Mary, who also sat at Jesus' feet and heard His word.*
>
> *But Martha was distracted with much serv-*

ing, and she approached Him and said, "Lord, do You not care that my sister has left me to serve alone? Therefore tell her to help me."

And Jesus answered and said to her, "Martha, Martha, you are worried and troubled about many things."
(Luke 10:38-41)

GOD'S PRIORITIES, NOT OURS

Martha's motives were good; she wanted to serve the Lord. But Martha's number-one priority was wrong. That is an important principle for us. To live your life for success, or money, or even for family or trying to do good things to try and please God with your good works—all of these are examples of the same strategic mistake Martha made. The Bible teaches us that God's decrees of how we ought to prioritize our lives are the exact opposite of what we naturally think.

What does God say our number-one priority in life should be? Let's return to Jesus, Mary, and Martha to find out.

THE ONLY RIGHT ANSWER TO THE QUESTION

Jesus said, "Martha, Martha. . .but *one thing* is needed," (emphasis added). What was that one thing? It was to sit at the feet of Jesus. Now that Jesus has ascended to heaven, how do we do that? We look to God every day by reading the Bible and spending time with Him in prayer. "Seek first the kingdom of God and His righteousness," Jesus said (Matthew 6:33). In another place He said, "And you shall love the Lord your God with all your heart, with all your soul, with all your mind, and with all your strength" (Mark 12:30).

You and I are called to live our lives earnestly longing to know what the Lord requires of us, and then doing it. It might hurt our pride to think of ourselves this way, but it's not far off from the image of a faithful sheepdog looking with unbroken attention at its master, eager and dutiful to act on his whistles and calls.

God is holy. Sovereign. King. Lord. Master. He is God, He dwells in heaven and does whatever He pleases (Psalm 115:3; 135:6). He created us. As His creatures He owns us. Therefore, we owe Him (and He rightly deserves) love and allegiance. Surrender and devotion. Loyalty and obedience. To violate God's commands is, as R. C. Sproul so eloquently put it, "cosmic treason."

But we can't obey God's commands on our own. Remember my illustration of our hearts being permanently out-of-alignment with God's will. Remember God said our hearts are polluted springs. God used the prophet Ezekiel to also tell us are hearts are "stony" (Ezekiel 11:19; 36:26). So, how can these out of alignment, polluted, hard-as-rock hearts of ours become aligned, pure, and soft?

They can't. At least, not by anything we can do about it. The only answer is Jesus.

The Bible makes it clear that you and I are sinful. We are morally and spiritually bankrupt. Guilty before God for having violated His commands countless times. God diagnoses our condition and tells us the terminal truth of it: We are dead in our sin. Our Judge has declared us sinners against His holy Law and now we are on eternal death row. There is no hope of reform.

All our attempts at turning over a new leaf and being

a good person will only end in failure. It is impossible for us to make amends with Him on our own. All our efforts to change and be a good person before God are piled up and considered only to be "filthy rags" before His pure eyes (Isaiah 64:6).

Our only hope is an Advocate. A Mediator. A Go-Between. Someone who is qualified to intercede with God the Father on our behalf. Someone who could take on Himself the punishment for sin we deserve. Someone perfectly righteous, perfectly morally pure. Someone infinite and eternal to take the infinite, eternal punishment for sin we deserve.

Enter Jesus.

Jesus is God. He existed eternally, one with the Father, and came down from heaven, born of a woman, fully God, fully Man. He lived a perfect, sinless life, fulfilling God's Law and requirements we never could. Though He was sinless, He was betrayed, arrested, tried, and sentenced to death. He was humiliated, mocked, and flogged with a cord made of strips of leather tipped with bits of bones and glass. He was paraded around like a party trick in a robe of mocked-royalty and a made to wear a crown not of the gold and jewels He deserved, but of thorns. And on a hill outside the city walls of Jerusalem, despite His perfect innocence, He was crucified, nailed to a cross of wood in the manner of a common criminal of the Roman Empire. Even one of the two thieves He was crucified between came to understand that Jesus was God, and so did one of the Roman soldiers standing guard at His pierced feet (Mark 15:39; Luke 23:39-43, 47).

Yet, He suffered willingly. "Father," He had prayed, "if it is Your will, take this cup away from Me;

nevertheless not My will, but Yours, be done" (Luke 22:42). Despite the wicked intentions of men, it was all part of God the Father's perfect plan to redeem undeserving sinners.

Jesus became the sacrifice to pay for the sins of all who would ever come to Him in faith.

Three days later He triumphed over death and the grave. He rose from the dead. He was seen publicly. He ascended into heaven. And one day soon He will return in full and final triumph to judge the world and establish His kingdom forever.

Because of Jesus' humiliation and exaltation, He has done exactly what He said He came to do: to free those captive in their sins, give sight to the spiritually blind, liberate the sin-oppressed, and declare the time of God's favor and mercy (Luke 4:16-21). Jesus endured all that He did so that all who would repent and believe this Good News could receive forgiveness from God for all their sins. Now He advocates before the Father on behalf of all who are His, those He saved by the shedding of His own blood.

But Jesus doesn't merely reform the wayward heart of someone who comes to Him for mercy. He doesn't correct our impossibly misaligned hearts like some spiritual auto mechanic. No, no! Like the miracle of Jesus turning ordinary water into wine, God does a radical new work in those whom He saves. He calls the dead to life. He takes out the stony heart and replaces it with a brand new one.

Then I will give them one heart, and I will put
a new spirit within them, and take the stony

~45~

> *heart out of their flesh, and give them a heart*
> *of flesh. . . .*
> *(Ezekiel 11:19)*

Without Jesus we have a heart in open rebellion against God. After Christ comes into our lives He gives us a heart, one that loves God and a new spirit that desires to follow and obey Him.

By the way, Jesus did not *suggest* we turn from our sins and believe the gospel; He *commanded* it:

> *Jesus answered and said to him, "Most assur-*
> *edly, I say to you, unless one is born again, he*
> *cannot see the kingdom of God. . . .Do not mar-*
> *vel that I said to you, "You must be born again."*
> *(John 3:3,7, emphasis added)*

If our first reaction to God's way of salvation is to try to redefine or run from what the Bible reveals about God and about ourselves, we've exposed ourselves for exactly what the Bible says about us. We prove that we hate God, we have no desire to obey His commands or submit to His rule over our lives, and we don't value at all what Christ did to save us sinners.

How do we know if we are truly "born again"? Remember the question we started this chapter with, *What are you living for?* We know we are truly born again by God when the motives in our heart and the confession of our lips reflect one declaration over all others: Jesus is Lord of my life.

> *We know we are truly born again by*
> *God when the motives in our heart and*

*the confession of our lips reflect one
declaration over all others:
Jesus is Lord of my life.*

When Jesus loosens the chains and sets free someone who was enslaved to sin and death, a miraculous thing happens: Out of profound love and gratitude he turns right around, falls to his knees, and joyfully *renounces* his emancipation. Rather than continuing to live for himself, he surrenders everything to be Christ's slave.

JESUS IS LORD OF MY LIFE

*Many who first followed Jesus were
the same ones later calling for Him to
be crucified. Little has changed. Many
people in our day also superficially
link up with Jesus. . . .*

It's one thing to profess to be a Christian because you live in a predominantly Christian culture; it's another to actually be one. For instance, I live in the American South, the area of the country traditionally known as the Bible Belt. If we were to head back out to the street to interview people, a lot of people would claim Jesus is Lord of their life. They'll say they are born again because of a church experience growing up. But if we could observe their lives, we would find out pretty quickly their lives bear no evidence of ever having an encounter with Him. They may have had a bit of religion at some point, but they were never born again by the Spirit of God, brought out of death and darkness into life and light.

It doesn't just happen in the Bible Belt. Many who first followed Jesus were the same ones later calling for Him to be crucified. Little has changed. People all around the world have had that experience, including me. Many people superficially link up with Jesus but that will never do. And it certainly won't do when they're standing before God on Judgment Day. Jesus calls those people liars and hypocrites (Matthew 7:21-23). If you want to be saved, you need to be born again.

Before you put your head on your pillow tonight, why not settle the matter for yourself? Ask yourself:

What am I living for?
Do I have that misaligned, impure, and stony heart, or do I have that new heart only God can give?

Better yet, ask God,
"Lord, make me born again by Your Spirit."

What Are You Living For?

NO FEAR

A lot of things in this world can claim to change your life for the better. And some certainly do. Falling in love changes your life, right? Getting that once-in-a-lifetime job offer is a big day in anyone's life. A grown man can be reduced to tears of joy the first time he holds his newborn son or daughter. But nothing in this world compares to the freedom God gives when He forgives sin and removes that ever-present, nagging fear of death.

LIFE SPEEDS BY

No two lives are the same. I was surprised to learn a few years ago that even identical twins have different fingerprints. But what unites us all is the inevitability of death. We're all going to some day, and sooner than we think.

As I write this, I'm now fifty years old. I can't believe I graduated high school over thirty years ago. The famous philosopher Seneca observed, "While we are postponing, life speeds by." He's right; I can't believe how quickly "life speeds by." Maybe you are still young and don't realize how quickly time passes. What I say may seem strange now, but one day you'll notice it too.

Israel's great King David was also a musician and a poet. In one of his psalms he reflected on the brevity of life. He wrote, "Man is like a breath; his days are like a passing shadow" (Psalm 144:4). James, the half-brother of Jesus, said much the same thing when he warned of the folly of making plans apart from God, "you do not know what will happen tomorrow. For what is your life? It is even a vapor that appears for a little time and then vanishes away" (James 4:14).

Does the idea of dying scare you? It should scare all of us. The problem is, it usually doesn't. We assume it is far off, so we push it out of our mind. Young people think it won't happen for a long time. By middle age they've been to enough funerals that they realize it could happen sooner rather than later. By old age many deceive themselves into not being afraid of dying. Theologian R. C. Sproul once quipped that the reason people boast that they aren't afraid of death is because they're not dying yet.

CAUGHT IN THE SNARE OF THE HUNTSMAN

There is a phrase used numerous times in the Old Testament, "the snares of death." For example, in Psalm 18 David writes, "the cords of Sheol [the grave] entangled me; the snares of death confronted me" (Psalm 18:5 ESV). That's a vivid description, but "snares" is not a word we use much these days, so we are apt to miss the significance of it. Bible scholar Heinrich A. W. Meyer helps us understand what the Bible is saying when he writes that "the snares of death" means that death is, "personified. . .as a huntsman laying a snare." Sooner or later each of us steps into one of its set traps.

The Cambridge Bible for Schools and Colleges paints the picture even more vibrantly, describing death and the grave as, "probably represented as hunters lying in wait for their prey with nooses and nets." Isn't that what death does? From the time we are in the womb, death waits for us. No matter how much we eat right and exercise, death pursues us. Eventually, it catches us. The older we get, the more we feel its cold inevitability.

> *To be afraid of dying is one way God confirms that little voice inside each of us that keeps saying: "There is a God."*

In the New Testament, the Apostle Peter used that same phrase, "the pangs [pains] of death." By "pangs," he means the pains or agony of a person bound and tied, helpless to escape. The apostle declared that death has that kind of hold on the entire human race, but God raised Christ from the dead, "having loosed the pains of death, because it was not possible that He should be held by it" (Acts 2:24).

FEAR OF DEATH POINTS US TO GOD'S EXISTENCE

God is merciful to warn us. He put the fear of death inside each of us for our own good. As surprising as it is to think of it this way, fear of death is a gift from God. For one thing, to be afraid of dying is one way God confirms that little voice inside each of us saying: *There is a God*. No matter how much we might say we believe otherwise, fear of death, like all of creation itself, is evidence that none of this exists by chance.

Under divine inspiration the Apostle Paul wrote that when men and women attempt to deny God exists, they are only trying to suppress what their conscience tells them is true:

> For the wrath of God is revealed from heaven
> against all ungodliness and unrighteousness of
> men, who suppress the truth in unrighteous-
> ness,
> because what may be known of God is manifest
> in them, for God has shown it to them.
> For since the creation of the world His invisible
> attributes are clearly seen, being understood
> by the things that are made, even His eternal
> power and Godhead, so that they are without
> excuse,
> (Romans 1:18-20)

In other words, there is no such thing as an agnostic or atheist, only people who refuse to acknowledge the truth their God-given conscience and the world around them confronts them with: *There is a God.*

> *In other words, there is no such thing as*
> *an agnostic or atheist, only people who*
> *refuse to acknowledge the truth their*
> *God-given conscience and the world*
> *around them confronts them with:*
> *There is a God.*

Let me give you an example of how this happens in most peoples' lives.

Back around 2016 I developed tinnitus (ringing in the ears). I have no idea what brought it on, but now I live with a constant shrill sound in both ears. Most of the time I don't notice it; the noise of life drowns it out. But in a quiet room, or if I wake up in the middle of night when everything else is silent, the ringing in my head fills the room, or at least *feels* like it does.

Our God-given conscience is like moral and spiritual tinnitus. It's constantly with us. But it's easy to go about our daily life, with all its noises and entertainments and distractions, and let those things drown out the ringing reminders that God exists and there is more to this life than meets the eye. The "natural man" as the Bible calls a person who does not know God, suppresses all the natural evidence for God. They spend their whole lives trying to block out the inward and outward proofs all around them.

FEAR OF DEATH POINTS US TO ETERNITY

Fear of death has another purpose in God's design. It also points us to the truth that there is something else after death, we don't just cease to exist. Instead, the Bible teaches us that God has put eternity in every person's heart (Ecclesiastes 3:11). We know it's there. Fear of death is the warning bell going off inside each of us that, *Yes, the Bible is right; I am eternal.*

Maybe right now you are reading this, and you say, *But I don't fear death!* There are only three reasons someone would say that. The first reason, as we learned from R. C. Sproul earlier, is that you aren't dying yet. When your final moment comes, you may. Why else do people plead for their lives when they are in mortal danger? The last words of Sigmund Freud, the famed founder of psychiatry and self-proclaimed atheist were a frightful lament of regret. Just before he passed into eternity he said, "Now, it is nothing but torture and makes no sense anymore."[2]

NUMBED TO THE FEAR OF DEATH

Another reason you may not fear death, the Bible says, is because you have chosen to live your life far from God. Consequently, God hardens the hearts of such people, cauterizing their consciences beyond feeling or caring, like it was "seared with a hot iron," (1 Timothy 4:2). In other words, God gives such a person exactly what they wanted their whole life long: no part in Him. When the end comes, that is a terrifying place to be.

The thought of dying and meeting your
Creator should scare you.
But it doesn't have to.

FEAR OF DEATH POINTS US TO JESUS

The thought of dying and meeting your Creator should scare you. But it doesn't have to. That's the third reason someone may not fear death: Jesus removes the fear, disarming death's power over a person.

Remember what the Apostle Peter preached that day in Acts chapter 2: Jesus removed the sting of inevitable, inescapable death, because He triumphed over it (1 Corinthians 15:55-57; Colossians 2:15). And now He offers to share His victory over death and hell to all who repent of their sins and believe in Him.

At this point, you'd be right to ask me if I have a

---

2 Psychology Today, "A Collection of Last Words." https://www.psychologytoday.com/us/blog/understanding-grief/201704/collection-last-words

fear of death? Naturally, I don't look forward to the aches and pains of my final hours, but Proverbs 14:32 promises, "the righteous has a refuge in his death." To be "righteous" means to be right with God. Someone who is right with God has the sure hope that when his or her time comes, God will be his refuge. Thanks be to God, He took my sin and unrighteousness and gave me *His* righteousness through Christ. So, whenever my time does come, I know without a doubt that God will be my safe place, my refuge. He will give me the grace to endure whatever may come and then He'll carry me into life everlasting.

Besides, those aches and pains are only going to last a little while anyway. Whether they last years, months, or only minutes, they won't last forever. The moment my body dies, the Lord has promised that my spirit will immediately be with Him forever. I am fully assured of where I'm going. I'm going to heaven to be with Jesus.

JESUS REMOVES THE FEAR OF DEATH

When He raised his friend Lazarus from the dead, Jesus proclaimed,

> *I am the resurrection and the life. He who believes in Me, though he may die, he shall live. And whoever lives and believes in Me shall never die. Do you believe this?*
> *(John 11:25-26)*

By the way, why do you think Jesus raised Lazarus from the dead? He called Lazarus out of his tomb after being dead for four days to publicly show that He is God and He alone has the power to give eternal life to all who believe in Him. The Bible says that "For the wages of sin is death, *but the gift of God is eternal life in Christ Jesus our Lord*" (Romans 6:23, emphasis added). Just as Jesus raised Lazarus up from his physical death, Jesus has the power to raise you up from spiritual death to spiritual life.

> *Just as Jesus raised Lazarus up from his physical death, Jesus has the power to raise you up from spiritual death to spiritual life.*

Not long after Jesus raised Lazarus from the dead, shortly before His own arrest, death, and resurrection, Jesus promised His disciples that He was returning to the Father to prepare a place for them and one day He would return for them to take them where He is (John 14:2-3).

These are not empty promises. Just like it wasn't an empty to promise to Lazarus' sisters that He would raise him from the dead. He did what He said He would.

I have no fear of *death* because Jesus changed my *life*. God, in His Word, has given believers many promises of the joy of eternal life with Him. He always does what He said He would do.

My certainty is all because of Him, not because of anything I did. All I ever did was sin against the Lord. It's all because of what Jesus did for me, His mercy to reach down and save me. Because He wore the crown of thorns on that day, all who turn to Him in faith will one day wear the crown of eternal life (Revelation 2:10).

How many of us can honestly say we don't fear death? Can you?

A MAN LIKE
NO OTHER

If you couldn't tell already, I am passionate about persuading people to read the Bible. Why? Because it is the only place on earth to find real answers, real truth. People can (and do) look everywhere–all kinds of religion, spirituality, self-help books, humanistic philosophies, and pop-culture celebrities. . . but all of those will fail you. "There is a way that seems right to a man," the Bible says, "But its end is the way of death." (Proverbs 14:12). They will fail you either in this life or the next, when it is too late to renounce them.

If we are to know God, to know truth, we must go to the Bible. When we read the Bible, asking God to open our eyes to its message, amazing truths will leap off the page.

The fourth book of the New Testament is the Gospel of John, one of the four Gospels. Together, they are more than biographical accounts of the earthly life and ministry of Jesus. They are eyewitness testimonies. Matthew and John are first-hand accounts and Mark and Luke are highly attested second-hand accounts. John was one of the three closest disciples (later apostles) of Jesus. I have read the Gospel of John dozens of times. In my last semester in seminary I read it every week for fifteen weeks. And still, every time I read it, I discover details and truths I'd not seen before.

The fourth chapter of John's Gospel tells the story of Jesus and the Samaritan woman at the well. It's a famous story of how Jesus intentionally brought the message of salvation, the Good News, to outsiders. First He brought it to the woman in His conversation with her, and then she ran and told the others in her village about this amazing Visitor. Look at the progression of who Jesus is perceived to be in John's Gospel, Chapter 4.

- First, He is observed to be, "a Jew" (4:9), one of a great multitude.
- But then he's called, "a Prophet" (4:19), one of an esteemed few.
- Third, He's called, "the Christ" (4:29), the promised one who would save God's people, Israel.
- Fourth, "Savior of the World" (4:42), not just of God's covenant people, Israel, but all of whom God would save and gather to Himself, from every tribe, people, and language (Revelation 7:9).

Also, imagine how amazing Jesus must have been to see and hear. After only two days, the townspeople came to a staggering conclusion:

They didn't think Jesus was simply *a Jew.*

They didn't simply esteem Him to be *a prophet.*

They weren't merely convinced He was the long-awaited Messiah, *the Christ.*

No, even greater than all of these, after being with Him some forty-eight hours, to a man and to a woman they concluded that this Man had to be none other than *the very Savior of the World.* He wasn't just Israel's promised Messiah and Savior; they professed He was theirs too. What was it about Jesus that had that kind of effect on them? The Bible tells us, and it wasn't what we might think.

WHAT ORDINARY MAN COULD HAVE THAT KIND SWAY OVER PEOPLE?

Jesus had no army. No technology. No clever sleight of hand or gimmicks with which to trick them. He did not travel with the awe-inspiring pomp that comes with descending the presidential stairs Air Force One.

The Bible doesn't tell us what Jesus looked like, except to say none of us would have given Him a second glance on the street. All we know is, "He had no form or majesty that we should look at him, and no beauty that we should desire him" (Isaiah 53:2 ESV). He had no outward charm or rugged good looks to lean on. Whatever He looked like, Jesus was so unimposing that children thought nothing of running up to Him. He was so common in outward appearance that when the Roman soldiers went to arrest Him, Judas Iscariot had to betray Him with a sign, so they knew whom to arrest, "Whomever I kiss, He is the One; seize him," (Matthew 26:48).

> *"In Him was life, and the light was the light of men. . .full of grace and truth."*
> *(John 1:4,14)*

The Bible says that when Jesus left heaven to come to earth to become a Man, He was fully God, though He left off His divine glory and made Himself of no reputation, took on the form of a slave, and was born in the likeness of men (Philippians 2:7). To look at

Him, there was nothing to suggest anything out of the ordinary. Jesus had no wealth either. All He had was Himself.

And He was Everything.

> *In Him was life, and the light was the light of men. . .full of grace and truth.*
> *(John 1:4,14)*

There were only ever two reactions when Jesus came into a town. Either He got the kind of welcoming reception like we started with, or the kind that ran Him out of town. Luke records what happened in another town, "Then the whole multitude of the surrounding region of the Gadarenes asked Him to depart from them. . ." (Luke 8:37). In another town he notes, "But they did not receive Him. . ." (Luke 9:53). In fact, in the opening of his Gospel account, John goes even further and makes it clear that *the world itself* did not welcome Jesus:

> *That was the true Light which gives light to ev-*
> *ery man coming into the world. He was in the*
> *world, and the world was made through Him,*
> *and the world did not know Him. He came to*
> *His own, and His own did not receive Him.*
> *(John 1:9-11)*

More towns and people rejected Jesus in His earthly ministry than accepted Him. Many of those early disciples who did follow Him would eventually turn back and not follow Him anymore. And of course, we know that it was only a matter of a few days before the crowd in Jerusalem went from singing His praises and laying down palm branches to shouting, "Crucify Him!"

NOTHING HAS CHANGED

The same is true today. Despite the overwhelming evidence, some people deny Jesus existed. Completely ignorant of the most basic facts about Him, they say that Jesus is a myth. But most people, and every major world religion, concede Jesus was a real person. They will usually concede He was a special teacher. Some may go so far as to honor Him as a prophet sent from God. But often they will stop short of saying Jesus *was* God.

But none of that will do. To profess He was a good Man, even a prophet, but not God, is as offensive to Him as to deny He ever existed. Both deny what God prophesied in the Scriptures. Both deny what Jesus said about Himself. And both deny the works He did.

Think about it. Is there a more supreme insult to God than to refuse to acknowledge who He said He is? To deny Jesus being fully God and fully Man is to deny both supernatural revelation and overwhelming evidence. To say that Jesus is anything other than God come down to earth is to call Him a liar.

If we pat ourselves on the back for believing that Jesus is God, but do not follow up with bowing before Him in worship and total surrender to His Lordship over our lives, we are insulting Him with worthless lip-service.

But there is another error we are in danger of making. It's a subtle one, too. Another deadly danger is to regard Jesus as exactly who He said He was—the Son of God—but then be content to leave it at that. Remember those Roman soldiers who arrested Jesus in John chapter 18? Jesus declared His true self to them, revealing His divinity, when He said, "I am He," (18:5). John informs his readers that in response to Jesus' words those hard-as-nails Roman soldiers "drew back and fell to the ground" (John 18:6). One would've thought that would make them think twice, but no. They experienced something of Jesus' glory and fell backwards, but then they got up and went forward with arresting Him anyway.

Are we any better? If we pat ourselves on the back for believing that Jesus is God, but then don't follow up with bowing before Him in worship, totally surrendering to His Lordship over our lives, we only insult Him with worthless lip-service. Jesus Himself warns such people, "Not everyone who says to Me, 'Lord, Lord,' shall enter the kingdom of heaven, but he who does the will of My Father in heaven" (Matthew 7:21).

WHAT IS IT TO "BELIEVE" IN JESUS?

We have already seen how John, in his Gospel introduction, says Jesus came into the world and they did not receive Him. John gives good news in the next sentence when he says, ". . . But as many as received Him, to them He gave the right to become children of God, to those who believe in His name" (John 1:12).

WHAT IS IT TO BELIEVE IN JESUS?

Millions of people would say they "believe" in Jesus, but the way the Bible describes it, it's more than just head knowledge or intellectual assent. As Bible commentator Albert Barnes defines it, to believe means to "put confidence in, rely on for support and consolation."[3]

> ". . . But as many as received Him, to them He gave the right to become children of God, to those who believe in His name" (John 1:12).

Individuals can only see and believe in Jesus by the Holy Spirit working in their lives. He draws them to Jesus. He opens their eyes to Jesus' Person and His power so they can see for themselves that Jesus is no ordinary Man, exactly like those Samaritans did that day. In saving faith, they, too, announce and confess that Jesus "is indeed the Savior of the world."

---

3   Albert Barnes, Barnes' *Notes on the Bible*. John 14:1.

Jesus Changed My Life

What would you say if we were sitting down together over a cup of coffee and I told you I had a life-changing experience? You would probably be a bit skeptical, and rightfully so.

After all, it depends on what the experience was, doesn't it? A lot of people claim that something or someone changed their lives. We tend to be dubious of such claims, and with good reason. Also, what is life-changing for you may not be for me, and vice versa.

That a thing is "life-changing" is the kind of claim we find almost everywhere, from TV commercials, to multi-level marketing pitches, and even religious cults. Advertisers spend millions of dollars each year hoping to convince us that buying their product will change our lives.

In order for a claim to be genuine, it has to be verifiable. It needs to be backed up with proof. What would be the proof that a person had a life-changing experience? *That his or her life was really changed.* To back up the claim there must be an obvious and permanent difference from who they were before.

JESUS CHRIST CHANGED MY LIFE

While typing this on my computer I did a quick Google search on the phrase "changed my life." Do you want to guess how many results came back? (Here's a hint:

Whatever you're about to guess, guess higher. A lot higher.) There are over 1.5 *billion* web pages that have something to do with life-changing experiences. With so many claims of being truly life-changing, is Jesus really that different than all the other claims?

Absolutely.

We've already talked about ways He has changed the world, but now I'd like to tell a little about how He changed *my* life. I wish I had time to tell you all the ways He's changed my life. Every day I'm a different, better man than I was the day before. In this chapter I want to tell you three ways Jesus has changed my life, and then I'm going to ask you to do two things.

No More Guilty Conscience

Since the Lord saved me from my life of cultural Christianity and religious hypocrisy, and made me a real, biblical, Christian, I wake up each day with a clean conscience. I have regrets about my former life, but I have no more *guilt* about it. Because Jesus paid the penalty for my sins in my place. Every ugly, sinful thought, word, or deed I've ever done—even those things I think back on and cringe thinking about—are all forgiven. When Satan brings them to mind and accuses me, I enjoy the peace of God's total forgiveness. When each day is over, I put my head on my pillow in peace. None of my sins have any power over me or my conscience anymore.

Can you say that? Does whatever system of beliefs or ethics or spirituality you base your life on give you absolute assurance like that?

I know it doesn't because I know it can't.

I don't say that in a proud way. I know it because before Jesus rescued me, I had such guilt and shame for what I had done in my life. I tried all kinds of philosophies to find peace and ways to silence my blaring conscience instead of turning to God. Some things worked to mask the symptoms for a little while, but nothing brought the promised cure. Nothing had the power to remove the stain of sin or to declare me innocent before God.

Why? Because I was going everywhere but to the Lord. When you are guilty of committing a crime and need to beg for mercy, you don't go to some place like the mall, you go to the judge and throw yourself on the mercy of the court. God is the judge of every man. All of us will stand before Him one day. When we do, we will not be judged by our standards of what is right, but by His. Only God can remove the guilt of our sins committed against Him and against others.

No number of good works can ever bring peace with God for so much as a single sin. The Bible says, "By grace you have been saved through faith, and that is not of yourselves; it is the gift of God, not of works, lest anyone should boast" (Ephesians 2:8-9). We can never earn God's pardon; it is up to Him to grant it. That's called grace.

God's grace is only available because of Jesus.

Let's go back to the Apostle Peter's sermon on the Day of Pentecost, when the Holy Spirit came and fell upon the believers, filling them with spiritual power. Look at how he widely and freely announces God's offer of forgiveness of sins now available through Jesus:

> *"Therefore let all the house of Israel know assuredly that God has made this Jesus, whom you crucified, both Lord and Christ."*
>
> *Now when they heard this, they were cut to the heart, and said to Peter and the rest of the apostles, "Men and brethren, what shall we do?"*
>
> *Then Peter said to them, "Repent, and let every one of you be baptized in the name of Jesus Christ for the remission of sins; and you shall receive the gift of the Holy Spirit. For the promise is to you and to your children, and to all who are afar off, as many as the Lord our God will call.*
> *(Acts 2:36-39, emphasis added)*

Jesus changed everything because He, as Lord and Christ, came to ransom from sin and save all whom God has called who come to Him in faith. He was crucified on the cross, He paid for the sins of all whom God would ever call to Himself with His own blood, died, and rose again.

The same offer is available to you today. "And to all who are far off, as many as the Lord our God will call," is for you, too. If you turn from your sins and turn to Jesus, you can know the joy of sins forgiven and peace with God.

JESUS IS REAL AND THE BIBLE IS ALIVE

Because Jesus changed my life, the Bible teaches that He now lives inside me, and I am "in" Him relationally. Since becoming a Christian, when I read about Jesus in the Bible, I don't see a character in a book. I don't see some one-dimensional historical figure. The Bible comes alive to me now.

I'm drawn to His kindness as He takes
a blind man by the hand and leads him
out to the edges of his village
so He can restore his sight.

The Bible has always been alive. God's Word declares of itself, "For the word of God is living and powerful, and sharper than any two-edged sword, piercing to the division of soul and of spirit, of joints and marrow, and is a discerner of the thoughts and intents of the heart" (Hebrews 4:12). Its truths are hidden from the natural person who doesn't know God (1 Corinthians 2:14). But now Jesus has also sent the Holy Spirit to me as He does for all believers. God the Father has given all things to the Son (Jesus), who in-turn has sent the Spirit to teach all who are born again by the Spirit to know God and He empowers us to obey Him (John 3:3; 16:13, 14).

When I read the Bible now, it's so real I can almost feel the breezes on the Sea of Galilee. I laugh when I read how Jesus uses humor to make a point. I'm drawn to His kindness as He takes a blind man by the hand and leads him out to the edges of his village so He can restore his sight.

Being a not-exactly-tall 5'7" myself, I can relate when I read about poor short Zacchaeus who climbed up a tree to get a better look at Jesus in the passing crowd. One of my favorite parts of Zacchaeus' story is when I read how Jesus stops, looks at Zacchaeus there in the tree, and calls to him by name, "Zacchaeus, hurry and come down. I'm having dinner at your house tonight."

I read about Jesus and it's like I'm reading a news article about something He did yesterday; and when I read it, I'm reading about my Friend. Jesus is as real to me as any friend I can call on my phone.

In fact, He's closer than that, He lives in my heart. When I am impatient and I snip at my wife, Jesus is there saying, *Anthony, you know better than that. Now go on, apologize to her.* He is as real to me in my life as if I could pull back a beautifully woven curtain and reveal to you a great hall piled floor-to-ceiling and gleaming with priceless jewels and gold and treasures. He is beautiful, kind, good, generous, loving, invincible, distant, and yet so near. . .all of these and more.

And yet, do not mistake His meekness for weakness. He does not suffer fools. He is patient now but one day He will rise up in righteous judgment to destroy His enemies. He is a "dread warrior" (Jeremiah 20:11 ESV). He is God. He is Lord. And He is my God. My Lord. He is my Master, my Creator, my Savior, and my King. He created me and He owns me. He "calls the shots" in my life, not me.

And He's the best Master you could ever want. He's certainly a better Master than I had when I was serving the devil and doing my own thing.

YOUR TURN

I told you I was going to tell you three ways Jesus changed my life and after that I would ask you to do two things. Now it is your turn.

First, decide for yourself if my testimony of a life-changing encounter with Jesus rings true. I realize you don't know me personally. You don't live with me to see what I'm like at home. You don't know how I treat my wife and others. You can't see my heart. But from what you can tell, is my life truly changed, or am I acting like a Madison Avenue ad agency, hoping to persuade you about how great some new brand of laundry detergent is?

Second, go back and think about your own set of beliefs I have challenged you several times already to think about. Imagine holding them out in front of you, inspecting them as you would inspect a diamond through a jeweler's loupe. How do your philosophies, your spirituality, whatever you want to call it, compare to Christ? Are they really worth holding on to?

WHAT IT MEANS TO FOLLOW JESUS

There I sat. Pen in hand. Contract before me. All I had to do was sign my name and my life would go a whole different direction. If I signed, minutes later I would be ushered into a roomful of others who just did the same, and together we would be sworn-in recruits of the United States Air Force.

What does my story have to do with being a Christian? We hear a lot about following Jesus. But what exactly does that mean? And what does it cost us? What of ourselves do we get to keep, versus what is His? Must we really give up everything? If so, why?

MY AIR FORCE STORY

I was nineteen years old.

I was working in the mailroom at a software company. I had no clue what I wanted to do with my life, so I talked to an Air Force recruiter. A week or two later and I'm up at the main recruiting and exam center. It's an overnight stay in a hotel and a day of physicals, interviews, and I don't remember what else. Then the moment comes. The contract is in front of me. In the second it takes to scribble out my signature I would be signing away the next four years of my life. In return, Uncle Sam promised me food, clothing, health care, education, benefits, discipline, direction, etc.

I stared at that paper. I was paralyzed by the reality

that it would still cost me four years of my life. My mind tried to count the cost. I seized up. Finally, I decided I couldn't sign it. I told the recruiters, "I'm really, really sorry, but I just can't do this." They tried to change my mind, but it was made up. Reluctantly, they gave me my commuter train ticket for home. I felt like such a failure on that train ride home. I cried and replayed the whole scene over and over in my head, wondering if I really did make the right decision.

Looking back, I regret not having gone into the Air Force. Four years would have passed in a heartbeat. But to my nineteen year-old self, it seemed like an eternity. Thankfully, while I can regret it humanly speaking, I can look back at that decision and trust in God's sovereignty about it. Whatever my thinking was at the time, the ultimate reason I did not join the Air Force that day was because it was not the Lord's will for me to go into the military. He had other plans.

AMERICAN "JESUS"

Too often in American Christianity, we're invited to follow Jesus, and the offer is sweetened by many of the same kinds of incentives. God will take care of us. God will give us peace. God will give us purpose. God will give us a job. Some preachers act like my recruiters, holding out all the benefits, and all you have to do is "sign-up with Jesus." Not all preachers. But a lot of what is passed off as Christianity in megachurches and on TV is a kind of huckster materialism, and oftentimes those buying it are professing Christians.

They profess to be Christians but they don't pray, don't read their Bibles, and likely aren't regular attenders at a local church. They likely aren't submitted under the authorities of God, His Word, and their local church leadership. If they were, they'd know better to avoid such teachings.

Consequently, many who come to Jesus through these hucksters and their gimmicks find out after the fact that following Jesus requires much more of them than they were ever told up front. And like the crowds who eventually cooled on their enthusiasm for Jesus and His earthly ministry, many pack it in and walk away. They aren't really walking away from the Jesus of the Bible, though, because they never knew Him to begin with.

WHAT DOES IT MEAN TO FOLLOW JESUS?

God does not want loveless obedience from us either. That is only dead religion. The cults and Roman Catholicism teach that sort of mechanical allegiance. One is taught to follow the institution as the authority, not the Bible. God hates that. He hated the vain religious worship of Israel in the Old Testament, and Jesus preached against the hypocritical religious leaders in His day in the New Testament. The Lord has much to say about loveless obedience.

In John's Revelation at the end of the New Testament, the risen and ascended Jesus had strong words of warning for the obedient but loveless churches. To the church in Ephesus He said "I have this against you, that you have left you first love," (Revelation 2:4). He rebuked the church in Sardis, "You have a name [reputation] that you are alive, but you are dead," (3:1). He told the church in Laodicea they were "lukewarm, and neither cold nor hot. . . wretched, miserable, poor, blind, and naked," (3:16,17). The Lord definitely has no use for dead religion.

I think of Mary's statement to the servants at the wedding in Cana, where Jesus turned the water into wine. When they ran out of wine during the celebration, the servants came to Mary to see what should be done about it. She, in turn, told Jesus. Then she told the servants, "Whatever He says to you, do it," (John 2:5). In simplest terms, that is also the crux of what it is to follow Jesus: We do whatever He tells us.

As others have wisely pointed out, following Jesus is to live with paradox. It is full commitment, but we can't do it in our own strength; we need the Spirit's power. It is to be completely free, and yet also a slave to the Lord Jesus. Followers of Jesus know the kindness of the Master and would have it no other way.

A DENIAL, A CROSS, AND FOOTSTEPS TO FOLLOW IN

I think of Jesus' rebuke to Peter, when He turned to Peter and said, "Get behind Me, Satan! You are an offense to Me, for you are not mindful of the things of God, but the things of men" (Matthew 16:23). Following Jesus is to have in mind the things of God.

The verses that follow Jesus' rebuke also help us think about what it means to follow Jesus.

Then Jesus said to His disciples, "If anyone desires to come after Me, let him deny himself, and take up his cross, and follow Me. For who-

*ever desires to save his life will lose it, but who-
ever loses his life for My sake will find it."
(Matthew 16:24–25)*

This denying self does not happen in our own strength. It's not like Jesus is saying we must live like monks, vainly relying on outward forms of religion. We deny ourselves by surrendering every ambition and possession we hold dear, even our very lives. But there's more to it than that.

Notice how there is one negative, "deny *himself*," but two positives? We don't do the first in a vacuum. We deny ourselves and fill that void with taking up our cross daily—the metaphor for dying to ourselves and our wants. And we follow the One who modeled it all for us when He denied Himself, took up His cross, and died for us.

Taken together, Jesus is saying that our heart's attitude ought to say,

*Lord, humanly speaking You know I don't want
a difficult life. I don't want to be ostracized for
believing in you, losing friends and loved ones.
I don't want to one day have to choose between
my job and my Lord. I also don't want to surrender my rights, deny myself of whatever I want;
those aren't in my natural character. But, You
are God. You are my God. Whatever You say and
wherever You lead, I will follow, so help me God.*

LISTEN TO HIM

And then a little while later at the Transfiguration, when Jesus revealed His glory to three of the disciples, we hear the Father say, "This is My beloved Son, in whom I am well pleased. Hear Him!" (Matthew 17:5). Following Jesus is demonstrating our love for Him by listening to Him and obeying His commands.

DISCIPLINING OURSELVES

Or it's the way Paul talks about how he disciplined himself, body and mind, to follow after Christ.

> *Therefore I run thus: not with uncertainty. Thus I fight: not as one who beats the air. But I discipline my body and bring it into subjection, lest, when I have preached to others, I myself should become disqualified.*
> *(1 Corinthians 9:26-27)*

We don't do these things to earn God's favor, or score points with Him. We obey because we love Him and have a new desire to live a life that is pleasing to Him.

For a man, that might be training himself to look the other way when a pretty woman is walking by or there is an ad with a pretty model. Any man or woman who follows Christ seeks to obey the principles He set forth, "I say to you that whoever looks at a woman to lust for her has already committed adultery with her in his heart." (Matthew 5:28). Why? Because Jesus is more precious to them than the sinful and fleeting thrill of a lustful thought.

REORIENTING OURSELVES

Following Jesus is a moment-by-moment reorienting of one's mind and affections on Christ and His will. Paul described it to the Christians in Corinth in this way: "[We bring] into captivity every thought to the obedience of Christ" (2 Corinthians 10:5). Here again, we can think of the example of lustful thoughts, but there are many other examples we can choose from: angry thoughts, jealous thoughts, covetous or greedy, selfish thoughts. . .

The natural person has no ability to control such thoughts. The person whom Christ saves is filled with the Holy Spirit, has a new nature, and renewed mind. He or she won't always get it right, but Jesus gives the power to take thoughts captive as part of obeying Him.

It is fighting against our human nature—what the Bible calls our "flesh" or "old man." When someone cuts me off on the road, I want to somehow get even. When someone hurts me, I want to strike back and hurt them double in return. When an image comes up on the screen God says we ought not to look at, our natural behavior is to keep watching.

Or maybe it is something as simple as I don't want to wash the dirty dishes that are in the sink. I don't want to take out the trash that's overflowing and needing to be taken out. If I leave it long enough, my wife will do it.

The true Christian is not a perfect Christian. Not yet, anyway. He or she fails every day. A true Christian still sins, but is grieved about it. That person repents and asks the Lord's forgiveness, and it is granted for Christ's sake and because of His shed blood. Then he gets up, with renewed strength by the Spirit, and presses on.

He keeps walking forward in faith and obedience, day after day, year after year, until the Lord calls him home.

Following Jesus is motivated by love, countering all that we naturally want to be and to do. We love Him, the Bible says, because He first loved us (1 John 4:19). It is devotion. It is uncompromising loyalty. It involves commands to do, but also commands to not do. It's always asking *What action or reaction would be most pleasing to my Lord for this situation?* It's humbling ourselves like a child and yet standing tall, battling as a soldier engaged in spiritual warfare (Mark 10:15; Ephesians 6:10-20)

Ultimately, following Jesus affects every area of our lives. Jesus becomes Lord (Master) of our time, our money, how we do our work, treat others, react when mistreated. . . The motto of the Christian is, in essence,

In areas of life big or small,
Jesus Christ is Lord of all.

What motivated me to do my job well
was the new heart God put inside me. I
knew God expected me to be faithful in
my work and do it as though
I were doing it for Him.

I'll give you one small example of how this plays out on the job. I've had jobs where they have contests. They might be contests for who sold the most, who closed the most tickets, processed the most customer orders. . . you get the idea. Because I was on the team, I was automatically part of these kinds of contests. Honestly, I couldn't stand them; I have never been a competitive person. The contests were meant to motivate us, but they never motivated me.

What motivated me to do my job well was the new heart God put inside me. How I did my work was to be a witness for Him, just like how in the early days of Christianity, those slaves who were Christians were sold at higher prices because they were more valued as better and more faithful slaves. I knew God expected me to be faithful in my work and do it as though I were doing it for Him (Colossians 3:23). I didn't need a contest; I needed to be a witness and an ambassador for my Lord.

Following Jesus affects our relationships and how we take care of those people, what we watch, what we read, what we listen to, how we spend our money and time. . .everything. Following Jesus means every area of our lives is under His Lordship.

FINAL THOUGHTS ABOUT WHAT IT MEANS TO FOLLOW JESUS

FOLLOWING JESUS IS OUR HIGHEST DUTY

All of us think about our duties towards our fellow man. All of us know, at least in principle, being a member of society means certain civic duties. We have a duty to obey the laws of the land—a duty to work as we are able and not be an undue burden on anyone; a duty to respect others, and so forth. Yet, we rarely think about our duty towards the very God who made us.

The Apostle Paul writes in Romans 12:

> *I appeal to you therefore, brothers, by the mercies of God, to present your bodies as a living sacrifice, holy and acceptable to God, which is your spiritual worship. Do not be conformed to this world, but be transformed by the renewal of your mind, that by testing you may discern what is the will of God, what is good and acceptable and perfect.*
> (Romans 12:1, ESV, emphasis added)

That phrase, "spiritual worship," is elsewhere translated, "your true and proper worship" (NIV) or "reasonable service" (KJV). As human beings, creatures created by God and made in His image, it is our duty to love, honor, and serve Him. Taken together, those words are often summed up in the Bible as to "fear" God.

Every human being's highest duty is to follow Christ. Why? Because He is God and we are not. He is worthy. He also commands it, and does so for our own good.

WANT TO BE "SELFISH"? FOLLOW JESUS

But also, become a Christian for your present and eternal good. Think about this: Suppose a person only loves himself. Suppose he or she is only living for himself or herself, and their only concern in life is *What's best for me?* If that's the driving motivation of our lives, then the irony is we absolutely ought to become a Christian since the greatest good we could possibly do for ourselves would be to surrender and follow Christ, because that is the truest means to happiness and blessedness in this life and in the life to come.

But also, it's about love and gratitude. Again, this is not about trying to earn God's favor or earn salvation. None of us can do that, anyway. Rather, it is out of love and gratitude for what He's already freely given us and what we freely received in Christ at the point of salvation. Let me illustrate this.

DID GOD BUY YOUR LUNCH OR SAVE YOU FROM CHOKING?

This is an illustration I've used many times when I try to explain to people the difference between American cultural Christianity, and genuine, biblical Christianity. I ask people: *Did God buy you lunch, or did He save you from choking?* Because a lot of times we treat God like He merely picked up the tab at lunch, when in fact He did infinitely more.

> *I would never forget how you saved my life and you can be sure I'd want to tell everybody!*

What I mean is, if you bought me lunch I would say, "Hey, thank you very much. I really enjoyed the time. Thanks for picking up the check." And I'd go on my merry way. I might tell somebody, I might tell my wife, "Oh, I had lunch with so-and-so today and they were nice. They bought my lunch." But I certainly wouldn't lay myself at your feet and declare my undying allegiance to you because you bought my lunch. In fact, that'd be crazy. After all, it was only lunch.

But suppose while we are having lunch, I start choking. I can't breathe and I'm dying. Suddenly, you come around and give me the Heimlich maneuver and save my life. I would never forget how you saved my life and you can be sure I'd want to tell everybody!

I'm also going to live my life in total gratitude for what you did for me. I would owe my life to you. In some sense, I'm always going to feel a debt of gratitude. It's not a debt that I'm trying to pay you back, but a debt of a desire, a debt to express my great thanks for what you did. On an infinitely grander scale, that's the kind of love and gratitude that motivates us, or *should* motivate us, to follow Jesus.

Is Following Jesus Worth It?

So now the last thing that I want to mention is, and the question you should be asking, is: Is it worth it?

A Thousand Times "Yes!"

Getting back to my Air Force story. Ultimately, at that point in my life, I decided it wasn't worth it. It wasn't worth giving up four years of my life for all those Air Force benefits. Do I regret it now? Yes. It would not have been nearly as big a sacrifice as I was making it to be.

What about following Jesus? Is He worth it? That is a choice we all must evaluate for ourselves. Jesus said that anyone who is considering following Him ought to count the cost (Luke 14:25-33).

My answer to you is a thousand times *Yes!* I've been following the Lord for more than fifteen years. Before that I was a false convert. I mostly had the kind of American cultural Christianity that treats God as if

He bought my lunch. I lived that way for twenty years before God saved me.

In the nearly twenty years since I have lived as a Christian saved by God's grace alone through Jesus, have been difficult at times, no doubt. I have been tested and tried and tempted in many ways. I have known joys that seemed like I was able to peek into heaven and I have known dark sorrows that plunged me into depression and despair. There are times I cried like the psalmist, "How long, O Lord?"

But still my answer to you is a thousand times *Yes*. And I'm not alone either. For two thousand years people have given up everything to follow Jesus. Some have lost everything, even life itself. And still they followed Jesus with conviction and with joy.

ARE YOU FOLLOWING JESUS?

What lasts in this world? Pleasure? No. Riches? No. Positions and success? No. If we really stop to think about who Jesus is and what He did to save sinners, there is no other way in this life that makes sense. There's nothing worth holding on to when we can have Jesus.

JESUS PLUS
NOTHING

Earlier we talked about our motives in life: *What are we living for?* As we consider that question, we also need to check our motives for coming to Jesus.

You've heard the old saying, "It's not what you know, it's who you know." All my life and career I've heard the importance of networking with others. When I was in business for myself, I attended business networking events where the whole point of meeting others was to refer business leads to each other. Maybe I knew someone who needed a good electrician, so I passed their name to Jim the electrician. Maybe Jim knew someone looking to buy or sell real estate. . . We were all networking in the hopes of growing our businesses through relationships.

It's always good to build relationships and help others. But there is a temptation that goes with it. We can be tempted to pursue a relationship with someone solely based on what we think we can *get from that person.* In other words, some people are just looking for a free lunch. Many times at those networking events someone would be all smiles and shake my hand when they thought I could be a lucrative source of business referrals, but when they realized I had no business leads for them, they turned ice-cold and moved on to someone else.

Jesus was well aware of those kinds of people. He encountered them in His day. In John's Gospel, chapter six, we read of Jesus' miraculous feeding of the 5,000 people who came to hear Him preach by the Sea of Galilee. (By the way, that was only counting the men; with women and children it was likely two or three times that amount, or more.) The next day, after Jesus has crossed over to the other side of the Sea of Galilee the night before, the same crowd walked around the Lake and sought Him out again. This sounds flattering, but Jesus was wise to the crowd's real motive.

Jesus answered them and said, "Most assuredly, I say to you, you seek Me, not because you saw the signs, but because you ate of the loaves and were filled."
(John 6:26)

They even talked a good bit of religion
to try to manipulate Jesus to give them
what they wanted.

Undeterred, they did their best to get another free meal from Jesus. They even talked a good bit of religion hoping to manipulate Jesus to give them what they wanted. *Rabbi,* they said, *Moses fed our forefathers bread from heaven . . .hint! hint!* (I'm paraphrasing here.)

Jesus wasn't having it. Instead, He told them that He Himself was the bread of life. If they wanted more bread to eat, He was the true bread that came down from heaven.

He told them to quit making the bread of this world—the bread that perishes—their priority. Instead they were to come to Him as the true, nourishing bread which gives eternal life. His words were shocking in their depiction of total commitment:

Then Jesus said to them, "Most assuredly, I say to you, unless you eat the flesh of the Son of Man and drink His blood, you have no life in you. Whoever eats My flesh and drinks My blood has eternal life, and I will raise him up at the last day. For My flesh is food indeed, and My blood is drink indeed. He who eats My flesh and drinks My blood abides in Me, and I in him." (John 6:53-56)

In the end, when they realized they could not manipulate Jesus to get more free stuff, they moved on. First they grumbled about Him (verse 41). Then they argued about Him (verse 52). Then they simply up and left Him, "From that time many of His disciples went back and walked with Him no more" (John 6:66).

Some things don't change, do they? Lots of people still come to Jesus because they got a free meal from Him once.

These people are the ones who were in a jam, some life crisis. They were desperate for help, so they went to church. Maybe they had a religious experience one time, crying and praising God during the service. Or maybe one time they got a helping hand from a church's benevolence fund when they were flat broke. Whatever it was, when their situation changed and they got out of whatever jam they were in, they went back to their old life.

Such people figure out that Jesus could help them, so they think they found a lifetime ticket on the Gravy Train Express. Some figure that if they talk a good enough streak of religion, they'll win Jesus over to get more stuff from Him. After all, *It's not what you know, it's who you know,* right? And of all the people to network with to "grow your business," or get something from—who better than Jesus? That's all terrible logic, but it's human nature. I know I was guilty of that thinking at times.

Let me tell you about a lady I'll call "Lori." When we lived in Louisville, Lori came into our little church in one of the poor parts of town (right across from the famous Churchill Downs, home to the Kentucky Derby). Lori visited on several occasions, and it was obvious she had real physical needs. As a church we rallied around her and helped her as much as we could.

One Wednesday night she asked our pastor and his wife for a ride, which they were happy to give her. She wanted a ride to the liquor store. Our pastor explained before she got into the car that, on principle, he could not give her a ride to a liquor store. She argued, but he held firm on the matter. He would drop her off anywhere else, but not the liquor store. She persisted. So did he. Once she realized she wasn't going to get her way, she got mad—Kentucky mad. She started yelling and cursing at him and cursing the church. Our pastor and his wife did drop her off someplace else, but she never did come back to church after that.

You might say, "I would never do that!" But isn't that the same thinking, the same heart attitude, of individuals who only go to church on Christmas or Easter, if at all? Or people who go to church regularly, read their Bible, but when the storms of life come, they are utterly shocked and unprepared because the "Jesus" they worshipped was supposed to only give them good things in life.

*Knowing facts about Jesus doesn't save
a person; genuine faith in Him does.*

The problem isn't with that old networking cliché. The problem is with our selfish, insincere, idolatrous hearts.

IT'S NOT WHAT YOU KNOW. . .

What a person knows about Jesus won't get them into heaven. Jesus told the crowd, "And this is the will of Him who sent Me, that everyone who sees the Son and believes in Him may have everlasting life; and I will raise him up at the last day" (John 6:40). Knowing facts about Jesus doesn't save a person; genuine faith in Him does.

It's not a faith that looks to Jesus for a free meal in this life or a free ticket to heaven in the next. Earlier in his Gospel, John records Jesus telling the woman at the well, "God is Spirit, and those who worship Him must worship in spirit and truth," (John 4:24). We must come to Jesus completely without pretense.

*Every person who desires to be saved
must come to Jesus for Jesus.
Jesus plus nothing.*

Every person who desires to be saved must come to Jesus for Jesus. Jesus plus nothing. No free lunch of loaves and fish, no health-and-wealth prosperity promises from the man (or woman) on TV. You must come to Him because you see God is holy and you are not. Because you are convinced from Scripture that

God is your Judge and you stand condemned, a sinner guilty of breaking God's Law your whole life long. Aware of your desperate condition, you see your need for mercy, for pardon, and for life, and that God is the only one who can give them. And so, you come humbly. Earnestly. In faith, believing that Jesus alone can save you.

You come like the dying thief on the cross, who had a change of heart about Jesus. He didn't ask for Jesus to save him from his execution, or even to bring him to heaven when they both died in a little while. But He looked to Jesus in faith, and as a result of that, gained eternal life in that hour.

It's been my point throughout this book to assert that *Jesus changed everything and, as a result, Jesus changes everything* when we follow Him. But it's also true that *Jesus will cost you everything.*

We come to Jesus for life, eternal life, and while salvation is entirely a free gift of God (Ephesians 2:8-9), it costs us surrendering our lives before Him (Romans 12:1). It makes sense that we who would take God's gracious offer of salvation, that came at the cost of Jesus' own blood, would then lay our lives at His feet, forever His grateful servants.

Maybe you are reading this and thinking,

> *I get it, sort of. I understand that God is holy and I'm a sinner, and only Jesus can save me because He died for me on the cross. I believe, but I'm unclear on a couple details. Before I go any further, where can I turn?*

Let me offer a few places:

PRAY. Jesus delights to bless people with good things. Sometimes they are those material things like a better job, but He also delights to bless them with spiritual things. Ask Him to lead you and give you faith to believe.

GOD'S WORD. A great place to start is the New Testament. You can start in Matthew's Gospel, the first book of the New Testament. Pray and ask the Lord to open your eyes and give you understanding as you read. He will. If you don't have a Bible at home, read it on the Internet, buy one at a thrift store, or just ask around. The Lord will make sure you get one.

CHURCH. Search for a Bible-teaching church in your area. Again, if you're unsure, ask the Lord to lead you. Listen for the pastor to read and explain the Bible plainly. Also, if you ask them, they should be happy to give you a Bible if you don't have one.

If I can be of help, please visit GraceandPeaceRadio. com. I don't have all the answers, but *It's not what you know, it's who you know,* and I know the One who has all the answers.

THE KING IS CALLING YOU

Turn to me and be saved,
all the ends of the earth!
For I am God, and there is no other.
(Isaiah 45:22 ESV)

Until the coronavirus hit in early 2020, I was on the preaching rotation of our church's ministry at a nearby nursing and rehabilitation facility. Every six weeks my wife and I would go there on a Sunday morning so I could conduct a small church service for the residents. Another couple from our church would usually join us to lead in singing hymns and playing the piano. It is a powerful thing to see a small group of people who have such limited cognitive skills come alive with joy to sing the hymns they've sung all their lives.

Usually only about a dozen or so of the residents would be in the main community room. Most were old, but not all. Some were mentally diminished. Some were physically diminished, but still had a gleam in their eye. And some were there in spirit but sound asleep. You never really knew who was listening and who wasn't, but that didn't much matter anyway. The point was to serve them with songs, with the personal touch of gentle handshakes, and with a short Bible sermon or devotional.

One visit my wife and I arrived early. The weekend activities director, Tom, was reading off the morning headlines with his own amusing quips and commentary. I remember when Tom was finished and

I moved to the front of the room to begin our church service, I said, "Well, you've heard the current news. Now you're going to hear the Good News."

We started the service singing the old hymn, *Jesus Saves,* which is obviously a song about getting saved and having our sins forgiven. When that happens, we have new life in Christ, the old has passed away, all things become new (2 Corinthians 5:17). We are washed. We are cleansed. We are born again (John 3:3).

And then from that point on in the life of every believer, we have *Blessed Assurance*, which is the next song we sang that morning. It truly is blessed assurance to experience the joys of salvation: sins forgiven, peace with God, and the sure hope of eternal life. That "blessed assurance" really is good news.

That morning I shared with them a sermon from just one verse in the Bible. I'd like to share that message with you as well. It's a message based on a verse from the prophet Isaiah. It is Isaiah 45:22. God is the one speaking and this is what He says,

"Turn to Me and be saved, all the ends of the earth, for I am God, and there is no other."

As is so often the case with God's Word, we have a small verse, but it's really packed with things for us to see. In this verse is the Good News of salvation.

If you're a Christian today, you never really move on from the basic truths of salvation through Jesus Christ. We mature in Christ; we grow in our faith, but we never leave the foundation of the gospel message, the Good News that is salvation by grace alone, through Christ alone, by faith alone.

TURN

The first thing we see in this verse is the word "turn." God says, "Turn to Me and be saved." First of all, let's ask: Who is the audience? To whom is God speaking this word? He says, "all the ends of the earth." So, this applies to all of us. The first word we see is "turn" and we know that God meant it for us, too.

That word, "turn" means that we're all going some direction, doesn't it? You wouldn't tell someone to turn unless they were going some direction. God is saying that in life all of us are going some direction. Some go to greatness. I heard in the news headlines that morning they talked about Jeff Bezos, the founder of Amazon and the richest man in the world. He certainly has gone a direction hasn't he? To go from an ordinary guy, like you or me, to become the richest man in the world. He is a rags-to-riches story.

Some people go to anonymity. They go from riches to rags.

One thing is for certain: we are all heading in some direction and God is saying, "Turn."

And there is one universal direction that all of us must go and will go. Of course, I'm talking about reaching the end of our lives—going to our deaths. Normally, we don't like to think about that. We're all facing eternity; we're all heading to eternity one day.

God says, "It is appointed for men to die once, but this the judgment" (Hebrews 9:27). What direction are you facing today? That's the first question that we can look at in the text and ask ourselves. What direction am I facing?

TO ME

The very fact God said "Turn" indicates we were not heading the direction that God commands and wants us to go. To say to someone, "Hey! Go away from that, turn around!" is to say that person is not heading in the direction he or she should be going.

So, what direction ought we to be going?

God says next, "Turn to Me. . ." As God reveals Himself through the pages of the Bible, He tells us the direction that we are going by nature, without Christ. God says, "Turn to Me," because Israel had gone the opposite direction, chasing after other gods and after sin. So has the whole human race ever since Adam and Eve first disobeyed God in the Garden and brought sin into the world. One generation after another after another, all going their own way apart from God. And so have we. That's why Ephesians 2:3 says "we. . .were by nature children of wrath." All of us are "children of wrath," enemies of God and His holiness, unless and until He saves us.

AND BE SAVED

We need to be saved. Romans 3:23 says, "For all have sinned and fall short of the glory of God." In ancient Israel's history, in the time of the Judges, it is described as a time when "everyone did what was right in his own eyes," (Judges 21:25). It was not unlike today in many respects.

And we say, "Well, that's rather harsh, isn't it?" We protest, "I don't want to be thought of in those terms." God shows us our true condition so that He can show us the true remedy.

The same word of warning from God Himself here in Isaiah applies today to every one of us, "Turn to Me and be saved. . ." Because the direction we're going naturally—that is, by our own inclination, is the direction of destruction. But God and His love and His kindness offers us the opportunity to turn.

God is saying the same thing to us when he's telling us the truth of our natural selves. So, God says, "Turn. Turn to Me and be saved, all the ends of the earth." The fact that God says, "turn to me and be saved," indicates that God is saying we need a savior. We need someone to save us. We are in a place in our lives apart from Christ, where we are dead—spiritually dead in our sins (Romans 6:23; Ephesians 2:1,5; Colossians 2:13). The Bible says we are stone cold dead in our sin, having no hope. God, in His kindness, is that Savior.

As we've already seen, our destination is coming. The Bible says there's a direction, "there is a way that seems right to a man, but the end is the way of death," (Proverbs 14:12). That is not just physical death, but spiritual death as well. Yet, God says, "Turn to Me and be saved. . ." God says, "nor is there salvation in any other, for there is no other name under heaven given among men by which we must be saved" (Acts 4:12).

Think about it: If you were drowning in the ocean and you needed a life preserver, and instead of throwing you a life preserver I threw you a cement block on the end of the rope, that wouldn't help you. If you were drowning and I threw you a tennis racket, that wouldn't help you. If I threw you a piece of wood, that wouldn't really help you much. And the fact of the matter is all of us in life at some point or another are grabbing on to things that won't help us. Those things are not saviors.

We grab on to things like riches or we grab on to our pride, our own efforts, and we try to save ourselves. "Well, I'm too proud. I'm going to dig myself out of my problems." We say, "I'll figure out how to get out of this sea that is drowning me."

We go to false religions. That morning in the nursing home I noticed on their events calendar that a religious cult comes in every Wednesday, teaching their false religion. They probably have knocked on your door. Maybe you took their literature. You don't want that. Their teachings are lies. They are only a cement block that won't save you from drowning in your sin.

ALL THE ENDS OF THE EARTH

God says there is only one way we can be saved out of our peril. The only way out of our danger is, "Turn to Me and be saved."

What a merciful offer from God! He doesn't want to leave us where we are. He calls to "all the ends of the earth."

This is an open invitation for everyone. For rich. For poor. Jeff Bezos can be saved. He can keep his wealth; God will let him stay wealthy. He can be saved. The poor can be saved. The young can be saved. The old can be saved. The healthy can be saved. The sick can be saved. Black can be saved. White can be saved. Asian can be saved. It doesn't matter who we are. A murderer can be saved. An adulterer. It doesn't matter what sins we've committed in our lives. A thief can be saved.

Or maybe we've led a good moral life, and we've never gotten in trouble with the law. It doesn't mean that we're all guiltless before God. Judge yourself by the Ten Commandments. See your guilt. If we've broken one Commandment (and all of us have), the Bible says we're guilty of breaking them all. And God is holy. So holy and just that if we only ever broke one Commandment—one sin in our whole life—we would still be guilty before such a holy God and deserve eternity in hell for our offense and rebellion against His Law.

It doesn't matter who we are. A murderer can be saved. An adulterer. It doesn't matter what sins we've committed in our lives. A thief can be saved.

But we can be saved. It's an invitation for the whole earth. God says, "'Come now, and let us reason together,' Says the LORD, 'though your sins are like scarlet, they shall be as white as snow; though they are red like crimson, they shall become as wool'" (Isaiah 1:18).

God counsels us, though we are wretched, poor, blind, miserable, and naked. He says, "Everyone who thirsts, come to the waters; and you who have no money, come, buy and eat. Yes, come, buy wine and milk without money and without price." (Revelation 3:17; Isaiah 55:1). That's the kind of generous God we have.

FOR I AM GOD, AND THERE IS NO OTHER

Again, what does God say in this verse? He says, "Turn to Me and be saved, all the ends of the earth." Who? Everybody. How? What does He say next? "For I am God, and there is no other."

Jesus said, "I am the way, the truth and the life. No one comes to the Father, except through Me" (John 14:6). Jesus Christ is supreme. He's sovereign. He's Lord, He's Master. He's Ruler. He's King. He is God. He's our Creator. He's our Judge. That should terrify us.

But if we go to Him for mercy, He is the one who forgives our sins because He shed His own blood on the cross, to atone for them, to take the Father's full wrath that's due for us. Jesus took it all upon Himself. What a kind and merciful, wonderful thing to do.

And yet, how often do we ignore His great sacrifice? How often we despise it and say, "I don't really care; I haven't cared all my life."

God in His mercy has kept you and me alive so that we would turn to Him and be saved. "There is no other."

When He says, "for I am God, and there is no other" that's two statements, isn't it? For I am God and there is no other. But at the same time, He's really saying the same thing. "I am God," and in that statement He encompasses everything.

There is no other God.

When God says, "I am God," He's saying I am supreme. I am sovereign. I am Lord.

Then he says, "There is no other." Think of false religions. Think of all the other religions in the world, and the thousands of other lowercase "g" "gods." The True God declares, "I am God and there is no other."

Remember the first temptation. The first lie that was told in the garden was, "If you eat of the fruit of the tree in the middle of the garden you shall be as gods." Oftentimes, the god we really worship may not be one "out there," but rather it's the one inside our own hearts.

> *God says, "Turn." "Turn to Me. . . ."*
> *Don't look at yourself. Don't look at*
> *anything else. "Look at Me,"*
> *He commands.*

God says, "Turn." "Turn to Me. . . ." Don't look at yourself. Don't look at anything else. "Look at Me," He commands. That word "Turn" is both a command and an invitation, isn't it?

It's an invitation to turn, like when Jesus says, "Come to Me, all you who labor and are heavy laden, and I will give you rest" (Matthew 11:28).

But it's also a command because God is the authority; we are not. *God* has commanded. God says that He had previously overlooked man's ignorance "but now commands all men everywhere to repent" (Acts 17:30).

That God would offer rebellious sinners salvation is remarkable. We certainly don't deserve it. It's Good News. What's even more amazing, more astonishing, is the means that God went through to make that offer available.

Isaiah prophesied of Jesus when he wrote, "All we like sheep have gone astray; We have turned, every one, to his own way; And the LORD has laid on Him the iniquity of us all" (Isaiah 53:6).

God Himself, in the Person of Jesus Christ, left all the glories of heaven and came down in the form of a Man. He lived among us without sin, and totally fulfilled the Law we couldn't keep. And though innocent, was condemned, died on the cross, shed His blood for us as the atoning sacrifice for our sin. That is astonishing.

"Turn to me and be saved. . ." is an offer, but it's also a command.

Mark opens his Gospel with Jesus beginning His earthly ministry, announcing, "The time is fulfilled, and the kingdom of God is at hand. Repent, and believe in the gospel" (Mark 1:15). That word repent means to turn, that is, to the turn from our sins. Turn and do what? "Repent and believe the gospel," that is, the Good News of the long-awaited salvation that had been promised, and now was come in the Person of Jesus Christ.

HAVE YOU COME TO HIM?

Let me close here with a question for you. It's a simple question. It's a yes-or-no question. It's not between me and you. It's a question you have to answer, one that is between you and God:

Have you obeyed God? Have you taken up His invitation? Have you turned to God? Have you repented of your sins? Have you acknowledged, "God, yes; Your Word says I'm a sinner and it's exactly right. I agree. 100 percent. I know I am."

Have you taken God up on his gracious invitation? Have you listened to God's command? Have you obeyed God's command?

These are yes or no questions. They're questions

that you have to answer for yourself in your own heart. You can tell me whatever you want. You tell other people whatever you want. You can even tell yourself whatever you want, and make yourself believe it. But ultimately God knows the real you. It's between you and God—just like it will be on that Last Day when you stand before Him in judgment. It will just be you and God.

> *These are yes or no questions. They're questions that you have to answer for yourself in your own heart.*

Today, through this book, I bring this Good News just like I brought it to my friends in the nursing home that Sunday morning. I share with you the same invitation I shared with them. And I plead with you to obey this command, just like I pleaded with them.

John 3:16 is probably the most famous verse in all the Bible and it says this:

> *For God so loved the world that He gave His only begotten Son, that whoever believes in Him should not perish but have everlasting life.*

That's the Good News. That's the hope you can have. God can wash your sins, cleanse you, and make you a new person. He can give you a new heart, the Bible says. He'll take your stony heart and give you a heart of flesh and put a new spirit in you (Ezekiel 36:26).

If you haven't guessed by now, I have one purpose in writing this book, and that was to tell you the gospel, the Good News. Why? Because

JESUS CHANGES EVERYTHING.

My message today is the same one in the first song that morning in the nursing home. It's two words: *Jesus Saves*. Do you know that today? I pray that you do.

Recently I listened to a man tell his story of twelve years of drug addiction and how Jesus set him free. That was twelve years ago, so he's now been clean for as long as he was using drugs. He had ruined his life but God, in the miraculous way that He does, reached down, saved him, and made him whole. God not only gave him new life. He gave him a story to tell, a testimony to share. "Come, see a Man. . . ."

Interestingly, that same day I also read the story of a professional baseball player who had become a Christian. This man had gotten "fired up" about Jesus, as the story was told. He quit all the vices of life on the road and was a changed man. . .but not for long.

> *He had ruined his life but God, in the miraculous way that he does, reached down, saved him, and made him whole.*

Years later, the writer recounting the ball player's conversion met him at a ballpark, where he was doing a meet and greet with fans. The writer waited in line while the player signed balls, hats, and having all the usual fan interactions retired baseball players do. When the writer got to meet him, he asked him if he was still "fired up for Jesus," the man lowered his head and admitted, "Not like I used to be." Whatever happened between him and his relationship with Jesus, the fire of that man's testimony burned out.

Many people would say they had the same experience. Maybe even you. The reason for this kind of spiritual burnout is something was in short supply. A fire burns because three things are present: Fuel, heat, and oxygen. Reduce or remove any one of those

YOUR STORY

Many of the Samaritans from that town believed in
Him because of the woman's testimony.
(John 4:39 ESV)

The story of the woman at the well is perhaps the most famous story in the whole New Testament of telling others about Jesus. For one thing, she not only shared about Jesus, she shared Jesus—running back into town to invite everyone to "Come, see a Man who told me all things that I ever did. Could this be the Christ?" (John 4:29).

It has been said of the preaching of Dr. Martyn Lloyd-Jones, a Welsh preacher in London in the twentieth century, that when he preached it wasn't like he was merely talking about God. Rather, people said that sitting there listening to him it was as if he went into a back room and brought God out and presented Him to the people. That's how vivid and powerful his preaching of Christ was.

FIRED UP OR TIRED OUT

I'm not a sports fan; none of it interests me. But, when I talk to people who are sports fans and they describe the players, the rivalries, or what is at stake in the big weekend matchup, I find their enthusiasm contagious. In that moment, I'm interested. When I hear people talk about how Jesus changed their lives, I stop and listen, and am fascinated by their stories.

and the fire will eventually go out.

I don't want to force the illustration, but when someone *used* to be "on fire for Jesus," it's obvious that something vital is not there anymore. That kind of person no longer prays. He no longer reads the Bible. People like this drift like tumbleweeds, in one church and out another. The crisis that drove them to their knees has passed. They feel they can stand on their own two feet again; they don't need the Lord anymore. Or maybe they simply decided, like Demas in the Bible, that they love this world too much to let it go (2 Timothy 4:10).

A GLORIOUS TRAIL

This brings up another point. If you spend any time at all in a circle of Christians, even a handful of them, pretty soon they get to talking about the Lord. And if you listen to their testimonies, as I have, you pick up on an interesting universal reality: Every true Christian's testimony about following Jesus Christ has some one or some thing they left behind to follow Him.

I can't tell you how many Christians I've talked to who, when you really hear their story of how God saved them, it includes how they were rejected by someone because of their new faith, or they gave up drugs, or drinking, or pornography, or anger, or it cost them something that was once dear to them. I've said many times that behind every true follower of the Lord Jesus Christ is a trail of this world's treasures, all of it forsaken *for Him.*

God does not call every Christian to be a preacher like Dr. Martyn Lloyd-Jones. But God does call Christians to tell others about Jesus. And it is fair to say that when a Christian tells others about Jesus, the listener ought to be able to detect a genuine vitality, a humble and grateful enthusiasm.

But what about when a Christian doesn't feel particularly enthusiastic? What about when life is hard? It is true that when we come to Jesus we are not suddenly immune to life's hardships. Christians still have good days and bad days. Although, ask any Christian and he'll tell you that even a "bad" day with the Lord is better than a "good" day without Him.

> *God will bring His people through times of joy and at other times may require them to pass through long trials. But through it all, the fire of a Christian's testimony never goes out.*

God will bring His people through times of joy and at other times may require them to pass through long trials. But through it all, the fire of a Christian's testimony never goes out. When a Christian talks to others about Jesus, they should sense a deep, humble conviction, a fiery internal glow, the way steel glows red hot in the furnace.

We all have a story. I'm sure if I had the opportunity to sit down with you to hear your life's story it would be fascinating. You may not think so. You might be thinking, "Oh, I don't know about that; mine's pretty ordinary." It is only ordinary to you because you are the one who lived it.

Throughout our time together I have sought to show in a very broad way how *Jesus changed everything*. Have

Your Story

Many of the Samaritans from that town believed in
Him because of the woman's testimony.
(John 4:39 ESV)

The story of the woman at the well is perhaps the most famous story in the whole New Testament of telling others about Jesus. For one thing, she not only shared about Jesus, she shared Jesus—running back into town to invite everyone to "Come, see a Man who told me all things that I ever did. Could this be the Christ?" (John 4:29).

It has been said of the preaching of Dr. Martyn Lloyd-Jones, a Welsh preacher in London in the twentieth century, that when he preached it wasn't like he was merely talking about God. Rather, people said that sitting there listening to him it was as if he went into a back room and brought God out and presented Him to the people. That's how vivid and powerful his preaching of Christ was.

FIRED UP OR TIRED OUT

I'm not a sports fan; none of it interests me. But, when I talk to people who are sports fans and they describe the players, the rivalries, or what is at stake in the big weekend matchup, I find their enthusiasm contagious. In that moment, I'm interested. When I hear people talk about how Jesus changed their lives, I stop and listen, and am fascinated by their stories.

Recently I listened to a man tell his story of twelve years of drug addiction and how Jesus set him free. That was twelve years ago, so he's now been clean for as long as he was using drugs. He had ruined his life but God, in the miraculous way that He does, reached down, saved him, and made him whole. God not only gave him new life. He gave him a story to tell, a testimony to share. "Come, see a Man. . . ."

Interestingly, that same day I also read the story of a professional baseball player who had become a Christian. This man had gotten "fired up" about Jesus, as the story was told. He quit all the vices of life on the road and was a changed man. . .but not for long.

He had ruined his life but God, in the miraculous way that he does, reached down, saved him, and made him whole.

Years later, the writer recounting the ball player's conversion met him at a ballpark, where he was doing a meet and greet with fans. The writer waited in line while the player signed balls, hats, and having all the usual fan interactions retired baseball players do. When the writer got to meet him, he asked him if he was still "fired up for Jesus," the man lowered his head and admitted, "Not like I used to be." Whatever happened between him and his relationship with Jesus, the fire of that man's testimony burned out.

Many people would say they had the same experience. Maybe even you. The reason for this kind of spiritual burnout is something was in short supply. A fire burns because three things are present: Fuel, heat, and oxygen. Reduce or remove any one of those and the fire will eventually go out.

I don't want to force the illustration, but when someone *used* to be "on fire for Jesus," it's obvious that something vital is not there anymore. That kind of person no longer prays. He no longer reads the Bible. People like this drift like tumbleweeds, in one church and out another. The crisis that drove them to their knees has passed. They feel they can stand on their own two feet again; they don't need the Lord anymore. Or maybe they simply decided, like Demas in the Bible, that they love this world too much to let it go (2 Timothy 4:10).

A GLORIOUS TRAIL

This brings up another point. If you spend any time at all in a circle of Christians, even a handful of them, pretty soon they get to talking about the Lord. And if you listen to their testimonies, as I have, you pick up on an interesting universal reality: Every true Christian's testimony about following Jesus Christ has some one or some thing they left behind to follow Him.

I can't tell you how many Christians I've talked to who, when you really hear their story of how God saved them, it includes how they were rejected by someone because of their new faith, or they gave up drugs, or drinking, or pornography, or anger, or it cost them something that was once dear to them. I've said many times that behind every true follower of the Lord Jesus Christ is a trail of this world's treasures, all of it forsaken *for Him*.

God does not call every Christian to be a preacher like Dr. Martyn Lloyd-Jones. But God does call Christians to tell others about Jesus. And it is fair to say that when a Christian tells others about Jesus, the listener ought to be able to detect a genuine vitality, a humble and grateful enthusiasm.

But what about when a Christian doesn't feel particularly enthusiastic? What about when life is hard? It is true that when we come to Jesus we are not suddenly immune to life's hardships. Christians still have good days and bad days. Although, ask any Christian and he'll tell you that even a "bad" day with the Lord is better than a "good" day without Him.

> *God will bring His people through times of joy and at other times may require them to pass through long trials. But through it all, the fire of a Christian's testimony never goes out.*

God will bring His people through times of joy and at other times may require them to pass through long trials. But through it all, the fire of a Christian's testimony never goes out. When a Christian talks to others about Jesus, they should sense a deep, humble conviction, a fiery internal glow, the way steel glows red hot in the furnace.

We all have a story. I'm sure if I had the opportunity to sit down with you to hear your life's story it would be fascinating. You may not think so. You might be thinking, "Oh, I don't know about that; mine's pretty ordinary." It is only ordinary to you because you are the one who lived it.

Throughout our time together I have sought to show in a very broad way how *Jesus changed everything*. Have

you caught a glimpse of that? What will the rest of your story be?

There are only two ways your story ends. Apart from Christ, all your sins *will* be revealed on the Day of Judgment. You will be made to give account. Without Christ's shed blood to cover your sins, you have an awful eternity in hell awaiting you.

The other choice is: Whatever has happened in your life so far, whatever you have done, if you repent of your sins and look to Jesus for forgiveness, He will forgive you. All of your past sins will be forgiven, even those private sins you are so ashamed of. The Lord knows about them all and will be gracious to every last one—past, present, and future.

> *Whatever has happened in your life so far, if you repent of your sins and believe in Jesus Christ for forgiveness and salvation from your sins, He will forgive you, cleanse you, and present you "blameless" to the Father.*

Do you call yourself a Christian? Did you have a go at following Jesus but, like so many others, eventually left Him when things got too difficult? Are you hanging your head in shame like that baseball player, no longer "on fire for Jesus"? If you ran into your town today to tell others about Jesus like the woman at the well did, would anyone believe in Jesus because of your testimony?

Let me close with words of hope. Throughout their history, Israel—God's chosen people through Abraham—were often fickle and faithless in their loyalty to the Lord. Over and over again the Lord sent

prophets to them to announce His judgment against them unless they turn from their rebellion and back to Him. Through one such prophet, Malachi, the Lord promised the people, "Return to Me, and I will return to you,' Says the LORD of hosts" (Malachi 3:7).

God's message to His people is the same for you today: It's not too late. Whether you never knew Jesus or you did a long time ago but your relationship with Him now is "not like it used to be," Jesus is patient and kind. The Lord's invitation is still extended to you:

> *Come to Me, all you who labor and are heavy laden, and I will give you rest. Take My yoke upon you and learn from Me, for I am gentle and lowly in heart, and you will find rest for your souls. For My yoke is easy and My burden is light."* *(Matthew 11:28-30)*

ABOUT ANTHONY RUSSO

For twenty years Anthony Russo was a nominal cultural Christian. That is, until September 2005 when the Lord soundly saved him. "I really am what the Bible calls "born again." I'm not who I was, my life and my heart are completely different. Selfishness, guilt, and shame were replaced with a genuine love for God and people. Jesus changed my life. He can change yours, too."

Since then Anthony has wanted to tell the world about Jesus. He is the author of several 30-day devotionals for *Anchor*, the devotional ministry of Haven Today, numerous blog articles, and the book *Pleasant Places: Reflections on the Christian Life.*

Anthony Russo is the creator and, along with his wife, Amy, co-host of the weekly Christian podcast, Grace and Peace Radio, available on your favorite podcast app, The Christian Podcast Community, or at GraceandPeaceRadio.com.

Anthony has an MA in Biblical Counseling and a Master of Divinity from Luther Rice College and Seminary. He and Amy live in Greenville, South Carolina.

CPSIA information can be obtained
at www.ICGtesting.com
Printed in the USA
BVHW041531301121
622873BV00011B/666